Short and Sweet

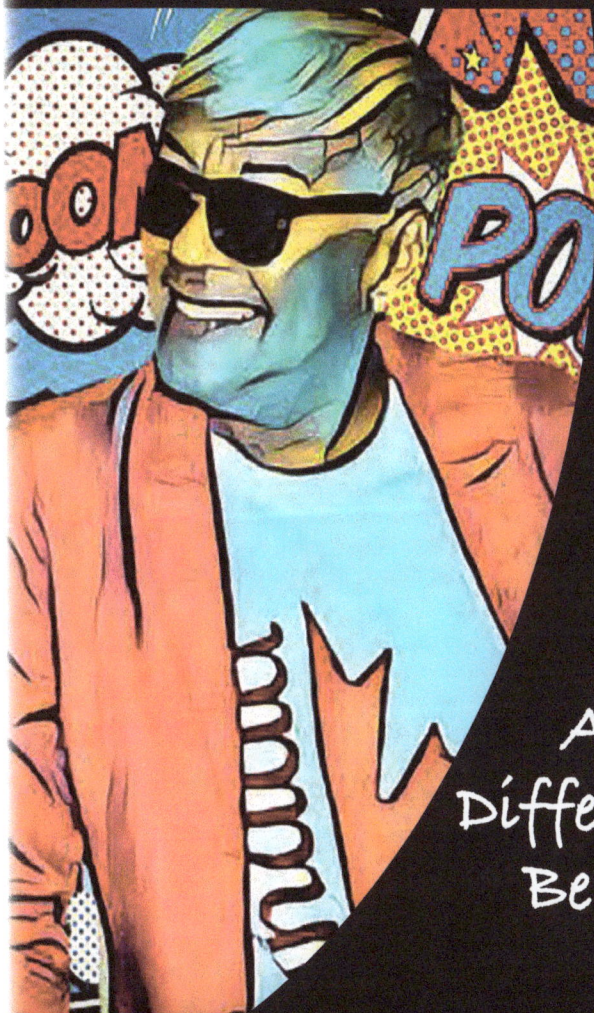

A Different Beat

Compiled and edited by Susan Cheeves King

GRACE

Grace Publishing House

Royalties for this book are donated to World Christian Broadcasting.

Short and Sweet A Different Beat

ISBN-13: 978-1-60495-057-1

If you enjoy

Short and Sweet
A Different Beat

you might also enjoy
other books in the *Short and Sweet* Series

Short and Sweet
Small Words for Big Thoughts

Short and Sweet Too
More Small Words for Big Thoughts

The Short and Sweet of It
When the Right Word Is a Short Word

Short and Sweet Goes Fourth

Short and Sweet Takes the Fifth

Short and Sweet's Family Album

Dedication

To my husband, Joe, an undisputed original

Table of Contents

Introduction

It all started decades ago when Mary Lou Redding caught an idea from a professor at Fort Wayne University. Further inspired by Joseph A. Ecclesine's "Big Words Are for the Birds" (at the end of the Introduction), she started assigning a one-syllable-word exercise in classes she taught at various writers' conferences all over the country.

Over the past 20 years, I have continued giving this assignment to those in my own classes. Writers at these conferences are motivated to learn whatever I can teach them about perfecting their craft because they know they're going to apply what they've learned, probably within an hour after they leave the classroom.

Still, they have come with the attitude that we who love to write all share. After all, we're writers. We love words. If a few words are good, many are better — especially the interesting word, maybe the elegant word . . . and definitely the special word only a particular writer can use.

And we do love to use the long, impressive words. But that can work against good communication. The truth is, the best communication is what the readers/listeners understand with the least effort — a Mr. Spock mind meld as it were — as if the ideas are just flowing from the writer's mind to theirs with no actual words involved.

We may love words, but if we use too many of them and ones that are not familiar and comfortable to the average reader/listener, then words just get in the way. Writing tight (saying a lot with a little) and using crisp, clear, accessible words in our writing and speech bring joy to the readers/listeners even if they may not know why.

That's good news for any of us who long for others to understand us, to hear us. The words we really should be using most of the time are already known to us. We don't have to get a college degree to learn them; we just think that we do. So we all need to break our attachments to those multi-syllable aliens that even non-professional writers/speakers tend to favor and get back to the simple words of our childhood.

The guidelines for contributors to this book in the *Short and Sweet* series were as follows:

ASSIGNMENT: Write about an original you have known using words of only one syllable. We are accepting non-fiction and poetry.

Although the themes are different, the following seven exceptions to the one-syllable-word-only requirement are part of the assignment for each book in the series:

1. Any proper noun is okay. (Don't lie. If you were born in California, don't write Maine; if a name is Machenheimer, don't write Clark.)
2. You may use polysyllabic words of five letters or fewer — for example: into, over, area, about
3. You may use contractions of more than one syllable such as couldn't, wouldn't, didn't
4. You may use numbers (even those that are polysyllabic).
5. As in any published work, direct quotes must be rendered word-for-word as they appear in the original, so their wording is exempt from the rules. This includes verses from the Bible—but only translations, not paraphrases (such as The Message).
6. Multi-syllable words for family (for which there are no single-syllable synonyms) are fine: mother, father, family, sister, brother, sibling, husband, daughter, etc.
7. Words for which no synonym exists — or at least no one-syllable synonym — such as college/university, geography, government, communication, heredity, politics, integrity, honest/honesty, person, regret, career/profession, passion, police, academy, education/instructor/professor, destination, hospital, institution, creativity, identity — or that cannot be replaced satisfactorily by a phrase of simple, one-syllable words.

If you're a writer — or aspire to be — and the challenge of writing in words of (mostly) one syllable intrigues you, why not give it a try? If you contact me at shortandsweettoo@gmail.com, I will send you the upcoming theme and deadline. You could be seeing your own work featured in the next book in the *Short and Sweet* series.

Susan Cheeves King

Big Words Are for the Birds

Joseph A. Ecclesine

When you come right down to it, there is no law that says you have to use big words in ads.

There are lots of small words, and good ones, that can be made to say all the things you want to say — quite as well as the big ones.

It may take more time to find the small words — but it can be well worth it. For most small words are quick to grasp. And best of all, most of us know what they mean.

Some small words — a lot of them, in fact — can say a thing just the way it should be said. They can be crisp, brief, to the point. Or they can be soft, round, smooth — rich with just the right feel, the right taste.

Use them with care and what you say can be slow or fast to read — as you wish.

Small words have a charm all their own — the charm of the quick, the lean, the lithe, the light on their toes. They dance, twist, turn, sing — light the way for the eyes of those who read, like sparks in the night — and stay on to sing some more.

Small words are clean, the grace notes of prose. There is an air to them that leaves you with the keen sense that they could not be more clear.

You know what they say the way you know a day is bright and fair — at first sight. And you find as you read that you like the way they say it.

Small words are sweet — to the ear, the tongue, and the mind.

Small words are gay — and lure you to their song as the flame lures the moth (which is not a bad thing for an ad to do).

Small words have a world of their own — a big world in which all of us live most of the time (which makes it a good place for ads, too).

And small words can catch big thoughts and hold them up for all who read to see — like bright stones in rings of gold.

With a good stock of small words, and the will to use them, you can write ads that will do all you want your ads to do — and more, much more.

In fact, if you play your cards right, you can write ads the way they all say ads should be done: in words like these (all the way down to the last one, that, is) of just one syllable.

About Joseph A. Ecclesine

Joseph A. Ecclesine was a Madison Avenue copywriter in the *Mad Men* era. He originally wrote this piece in the 1960s for other copywriters.

A shorter version titled "Words of One Syllable," ran in *Reader's Digest.*

These two versions have also appeared in various other publications while being used as inspirational models for college writing courses around the country.

Born in Boston, Ecclesine graduated from Fordham University in 1929, months before the stock market crash that triggered the Great Depression. He was fortunate to find work at the *Bronx Home News* during that period. He later worked in the press department of NBC in Manhattan, where he met his future wife, Margy, also a writer there.

They celebrated more than 50 years of marriage and had eight children. While living in New York, he worked at several major ad agencies and became promotion director of *Look Magazine.*

His catchy headlines and prose could be found in the campaigns of numerous companies, including IBM, National Geographic, Revlon and American Airlines. He also wrote fiction and essays, with a 1930s piece in *Esquire* magazine, followed by work in *The New Yorker, Newsweek* and *Short Story International.* He had an innate curiosity about everything, which translated into an extreme zest for life.

An accomplished watercolorist, Ecclesine allegedly sold his first piece to boxer Gene Tunney, who held the world heavyweight championship in the late 1920s. Ecclesine's watercolors were featured in *The Artist* magazine, and he had a one-man show during his retirement in San Diego. While living in California during his final years, he taught courses in memoir writing for senior citizens in a continuing education program at UCSD (University of California at San Diego).

1

Under New Rule

Patricia Huey

On that first day of math class, I sulked in my seat at the back of the room. The hot June day warmed the air, but the sweat beads formed from my angst. As usual, I'd strived to make good grades, and 9th grade was fine except for Algebra I. My irked dad had said I was to take the class over and bring up the grade. I knew better than to argue.

The door banged open. A young school coach breezed in, dressed in khaki slacks and a sports shirt. He flashed a smile.

A coach for math?

"Hello, class! I'm Coach Ryan. You're here to learn, so let's begin!" He called roll then moved on to class rules. Show up on time. Do all the work. What he said next, though, jerked me out of my slump.

"It's okay to goof. If you do, I'll know how to help you. And it's okay to chew gum. It eases stress. Just don't stick it under the table. I'll be sure to check."

Who cares about gum? I hate math! His keen, dark eyes bored through me. *Can he read my mind?* "You might think you hate math, but you must learn it. I hope you begin to like it."

Fat chance.

"If you abide by my rules, in six weeks you'll know Algebra I, and your low math grade? It'll fade away."

For real? I sat up.

"I bet you have the basic idea, but I'll help you hone your skills. You'll learn rules, steps, and logic. Like any sports game."

Math is not a game.

I thought back to the school year and my then Algebra I teacher. She loved to call people to the board. "Solve this!" she would boom. The scared student would try her best, but fear numbed her brain. She called up a boy. "Do this one! Quick!" The kid tried, but one missed step caused wrath. I shrank up small. Maybe she wouldn't see me.

"Miss Breland! Please go to the board!" Coach Ryan tossed his chalk to me. I dropped it. *Great.* I trudged to the board, weak and dizzy.

"Solve this." I tried my best, but my old issues cropped up: fear and brain fog. "Hmmm." He ran his hand through his short hair. "Watch this."

Coach Ryan picked up a piece of chalk with his left hand, tossed it to his right, and then back again. He dropped it, kicked it high into the air, and with one small pivot, caught it in his left hand! First, he wrote an equal sign, then, on the left side, he wrote a digit next to an x, plus one other digit. Next, he tossed the chalk to a kid in the back of the room just to wake him up, then told the kid to toss it back. The coach caught it with his right hand, wrote more digits on the right side, the awed class at full focus.

"What's done on one side must be done on the other, but be sure to change the sign." Then he grabbed more chalk, and with his left hand wrote steps on the left side, while his right hand wrote steps on the right side. He had solved for x!

"Model what I just did." I froze. *Write with both hands?* "Focus on one step at a time." He waved as if we were at the start of a race.

Hope began to rise above the fog. This teacher was not like any I had ever known. The old teacher's rule was over. I was under new rule, and I liked it. That day, my fear walked out the door.

I did the math.

"You have one issue." It was a dare, not a taunt. "Take your time." The room stayed dead quiet. While I thought, he rocked from his heels to his toes — ever on the move.

I scanned his math steps, saw the glitch, and fixed it. Coach Ryan grinned. "Way to go! How many of you at your desks got it?" Hands shot up. Coach reached into his desk and pulled out gum. He aimed as if at a hoop. If you dropped it, you went to the board. Lots of kids dropped theirs. Coach Ryan liked to throw things, but he didn't seem to throw fits.

Over the six weeks of class, he made math fun, but he wasn't easy. We played on teams and kept score. He was his own team and hard to beat, but we gave it our best shot. He jogged in place and told us it was okay if we jogged, too, if it helped us think. He taught us step by step and warned us not to skip a step. Skipped steps were fouls. He taught us how to F.O.I.L. First, outer, inner, last. Because we used what we learned, the rules stuck. After class, it took hours to get the work done, but not one kid whined.

One day on a rare break, my peers and I talked about our other math teacher. Our words vexed Coach Ryan. He marched over.

"Look, team, I agree she's tough, but she knows math. And you learned from her! Look how far you've come in four weeks! Don't look back, kids. Aim to win."

"The Coach Ryan Model" worked. He didn't just teach math. Coach Ryan taught how to set goals, how to work hard, how to win, and how to think apart from the crowd. He earned my favor, and I'm proud to say I earned his, along with a new frame of mind, and a great math grade — the old one wiped clean.

2

The Stained-Glass Encounter

Karen O. Allen

The church was lit by the sun at dusk as it shone through the stained glass. Hues of red, green, and blue danced over the room. My husband and I were late and slipped in to find a seat on one of the back pews. I saw a young girl near us whom I had not seen in church. She was alone. I glanced at her a few times but did not dare meet her eyes. On the last hymn, she saw me sing with no book in my hands and pegged me as "the token one." After the last "Amen," she moved toward me. I shirked. "Would you be so kind as to pray with me please?" she asked. "I'd be glad to," I said, though in my heart I had both joy and fear.

Her eyes were dark, her voice soft, and her frizzed hair looked as if it had not been brushed all day. She wore blue jeans and a long-sleeved plaid shirt over a tee. Her name was Sharon. She seemed fraught and in search of a friend. She told me that the stained glass had drawn her to come in to check it out. *I guess that's good she came to a church to seek help,* I thought, *but why did she choose me? I don't even pray that well! Heck, I don't even like to pray out loud. God, what are you up to?*

I took Sharon to our prayer room. We talked for a while, then both of us kneeled as I prayed. I didn't know what to say, but God led my words. After the prayer, Sharon still seemed tense and didn't want me to leave, but I knew that by that time, I would be missed. In fact, I later found out that my husband and a friend had been in search of me for a while.

As we walked toward the door, Sharon asked if I would teach her more about being a pupil of Christ. I had never been asked such a thing but leapt at the thought. *I could come up with a plan*, I mused. *It would be fun.* I told her we could try and see how it went. When she asked how often and what days she could call me, I wasn't sure I had made the right choice. *Who was this strange girl? An angel? A demon?* We met the next week, then the next and the next. We clicked as friends, but I was still wary. For some time I had prayed that God would send me a friend with whom I could share life's joys and talk about His touch. Sharon was not like any friend I had ever known. Her thoughts were out of the box. Dark at times. Her life had been full of chaos, yet she had a calm about her. An only child, she told me of a life that was like one big blur of bleak days mixed with a few good ones. Her parents seemed messed up, too, but at least they took her to church. Sharon said her Mom placed her on the altar to be blessed soon after she was born. Sharon knew about Jesus but had doubt about Abba Father since her Dad was not a good role model. The first time I met her Dad was at the ER when Sharon tricked him to bring him in for psych tests.

In Sharon's life friends tend to come and go, but I have stayed. I've stayed when her moods were so bad that she drove far away to seek help but failed to tell me. My phone has rung off the hook as I tried to find her . . . more than once. I've stayed when she lived in her car for a while. I've stayed when she called me at all hours of the night and showed up at my door. But I have also stayed to watch her get on her feet and do more than live through the day. I've stayed to see God work in ways I'd not known. I've stayed to see her shine through her art. And I've stayed to see her dark eyes turn brown.

Twenty years have passed since that first prayer on a cold February night. Sharon and I have dredged through much pain and grief, but our sweet bond has been worth it all. Sharon has taught me more about life than I could ever have learned on my own. She has forced me to open my eyes a bit wider. Even though she says I taught her how to love and not act like a stiff, rigid tree when hugged, she is the one who taught me how to love through thick and thin. I also learned to use tough love when the need arose.

God's hand of grace has been with us and has shown us both how to grow through hard times. We've shared the loss and joys of health, jobs, deaths, births, school, aches and pains, friends, and more. We laugh at God's humor that brought each of us into the life of the other under that stained-glass. Ever since her Mom died years ago, Sharon has dubbed me her God-mother. I think it fits quite well since I view her as a daughter as well as a friend.

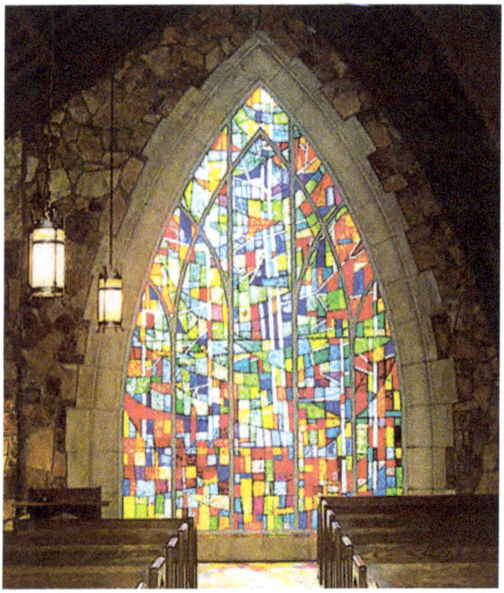

Of all the folks in this wide world, I am in awe how God chose Sharon — a laid-back, Type B, hit-or-miss kind of girl — for me, an It-All-Has-a-Place, Type A, get-it-done girl. He knew just what He was doing. Turns out God picked me for her, too. Sharon had prayed for a friend to teach her.

God's Word says He has His ways and they are not like ours. How well we two know this to be true!

3

Not Mr. Perfect

Bonnie Culp

She's good lookin: great body, very classy, smooth, nice rear end, perky headlights, in great shape, purrs like a kitten." I should have been flattered, embarrassed, or alarmed. But, knowing my husband, Al, as I did, I could infer that he was talking about a car. He had a thing for cars. In fact, he was buying, trading, and selling them so fast no one could ever be sure what car we'd drive up in.

While his soft spot was for cars, I was into home decor parties. Tupperware, Princess House. You name it, I bought it. It's not that we had a lot of money. We lived paycheck to paycheck, but our tacit motto was "Que sera, sera. What will be will be" — live and let live. This is what happens when two second-to-the-youngests marry. With many older siblings always coming to our rescue, we never had to worry about stuff. Always going and doing was fun . . . and we went and did — a lot.

I once heard it said, "Bonnie and Al have the perfect marriage." If perfect means never budgeting, not communicating, occasional empty cupboards, flying by the seat of our pants and that sort of thing — then yes, we had the perfect marriage.

However, this sort of life can't go on forever. And one day it came to a rapid halt. Al always had a thing for Ford Mustangs, and he had bought several before he found this particular one — not by accident, but because he scoured dealerships constantly. On this day, he thought he would do me a favor by selling my car and buying a "better" one. He sold my much-loved Toyota Supra without asking me. (I have noted that we didn't always communicate.) My Supra was so cool and sleek and easy to handle, and fun to drive. Before car seats were a law my little two-year-old Jody would sit right next to me on the console, she loved sitting up there looking out the front window. I'd slam on the brakes, she would fall to the floorboard, I'd pick her up, put her back on the console and we'd be on our way. (I never said I was the sharpest crayon in the box.)

I digress. Anyway getting back to Al — he planned to get this new car, so he drove there in one car and found himself with two cars to drive home. He knew he could not ask me to help him out; I was a little ticked at him. So, he drove them both home. He would drive one so far, park it and run back to get the other one, then drive that past the first car. That way he leap frogged them all the way home. It had to be at least 5 miles.

A few days later he came home from work and found an empty house. I had called a consignment shop to come and pick up all of our furniture. He looked a little stunned and asked, "Why?" I replied, "I just don't like that style anymore."

Do you know, he never bought and sold cars after that. He drove and kept that Mustang for nearly 20 years. I would like to say it was due to my savvy plan, but in reality, the cost of cars had gone up too much. What had been a couple hundred here or there became thousands, and he lost too much. But, he did like to shop cars with our girls, and he made sure their cars were always clean and running well.

They both had Mustangs.

If I could give a bit of advice to young marrieds, I would say, "Don't bail out when he or she is no longer that perfect person. Stay with it and things will work themselves out. Have fun together, pray together and make decisions together."

We were married for 36 years, and it was death that parted us. In one fell swoop, I lost my best friend, my faithful cheerleader, my co-celebrator of life, my memory maker, my perfect partner.

I like to think he is in heaven driving on those streets of gold.

4

Erica

Rachel Lulich

She laughs and the world bursts open
wide-eyed at the noise —
a gust, a snort, a surge of sound
with quiet breaks and shakes and all the while
we laugh with her and laugh at her and stare and point,

bold with glee and shock and joy
that such a show should exist on earth
in one so quick
to feel all things both good and bad alike
and not hold back; she lets us know;
storms and calms like an Indiana spring.

She has no chill.

You might think it odd or frown
at her lack of self-rule, but you would be wrong.
She'll face her fears and ride through gloom
and when she's mad she's mad —
but not for long.
Alone among the feels, her joy has no limit.

Her mirth could break the Queen's Guard.

5

Dear Miss Agler . . .

Judee Stapp

I stood still with one foot on top of the other while my third-grade teacher read my assignment. She had made me write it for the fourth time. I held my breath until she smiled and put her hand on my arm. "This is a good story now, Judee," she said as she looked at me over her specs. "The way you began the piece is better now, and your script is interesting."

Coming from Miss Agler, this was high praise. She urged her kids to do their best, with the sky as our only limit. For a child like me, who didn't get praise at home, Miss Agler had become my muse.

"Thank you, Miss Agler!" I felt as if I could float back to my seat.

I got almost no attention at home. I was born when my brother was 13 and my sister 10. My folks thought they were through having kids. I wasn't harmed — just not seen and so left on my own. It felt as if Miss Agler had stepped into my life just to fill that void in my heart.

Miss Agler was a force of nature — a fact belied by her prim, five-foot frame and "sensible shoes." As she taught reading, English, grammar, and cursive writing, she also taught us to respect adults and each other. Her core class rules to be on time and take turns gave me guides to live by that I didn't get at home. She always said, "Good, better, best. Don't rest until your good is better and your better is best." I grew to love her very much and worked hard in school to please her. I was so proud to be the first child to earn all As in Miss Agler's class.

I think I may have filled an empty space in her life as well. Miss Agler had never wed and gave her life to her students. She urged me to stick to my dream of writing.

When I was in fifth grade, my parents moved to Utah. So sad that I had to leave Miss Agler, I sobbed in her arms; and she vowed to write.

When my folks sent me to a girls' school in Salt Lake City, I felt so lost. I had to ride a Greyhound bus 25 miles to school and then walk about two miles. At ten years old, I was scared I might go to sleep on the bus and wake up in Wyoming!

Miss Agler told me to take notes about those I met on the trip and put them in my stories. I wrote lots of stories and sent them all to her, one by one. Each week, she wrote to me and gave me hints to spice up my work.

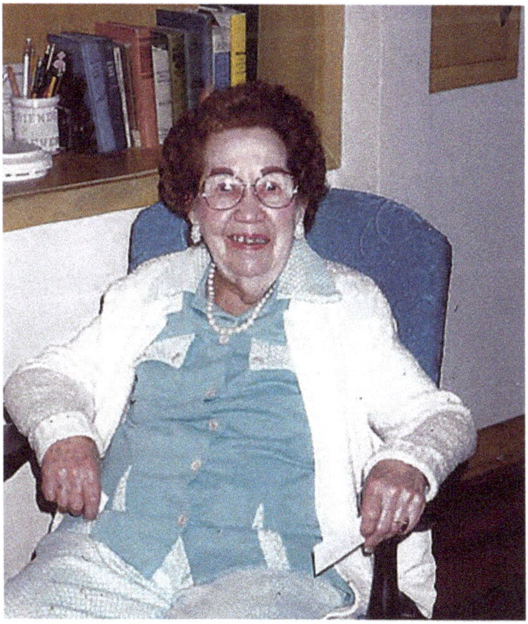

Then in mid-eighth grade, my parents moved to California and once more I was thrown into a school where I knew no one. Miss Agler wrote and urged me to "make a friend, be a friend, and make notes for your writing."

Instead, I married at 18 and soon had two kids. I didn't write any stories for a long time. I did send her snaps of my kids as they grew and were in dance and band. Later, I sent her pics of my grandchildren. When any of us won a prize or praise, Miss Agler was the first one I told.

In what I came to think of as her "love mail" she began to urge me to start school once more. So, I went to college over a span of 15 years — one class at a time. Without her faith in me, I don't think I would have graduated. I wished she could have been there, but I sent pics and she wrote back, "How great! I am SO proud of you!" I felt the same as I had as a kid when she would pat my arm and say, "Well done."

In 2003, I went back to Nebraska to see Miss Agler. As I drove up to the small house, the past filled my mind and heart. At the door, she was there to greet me with her big smile. I ran up the walk into her hug. She was so small. She walked with a cane, but her smile and her kind eyes were the same. Even though she was 92 and had retired from teaching, Miss Agler's mind was still sharp as she ran the town library.

She had tea laid out for us and as I sat down with her, my eyes were drawn to the wall behind her with its hundreds of pictures of her students over the years — as kids and then with their own kids and even their grandchildren. She had kept in touch with them all. She also had kept all my stories in a cupboard and pulled out one after the other to show me. "Please take them home with you and make a book out of them," she told me. Tears ran down my face as I took them from her.

That day I sat in Miss Agler's front room in her small house, as she served me tea in her best cups, worn from long use. I looked at the faded chairs and the rag floor rugs. She hadn't earned much through teaching, and she had lived alone most of her life. Miss Agler could not fund her dream to travel but toured the world through her books and maps. By most people's gauge, she had no fame. Yet she meant so much to me and the rest of her students, her loving friends, and her church. She was happy with her life.

When I looked at her wall of memories, I realized that one little woman can leave a very big mark on the world — one person at a time. "Good, better, best. Never rest until your good is better and your better is best." When I got home, I started writing again.

Though my dear teacher lived only four years after that visit, she will live on in the minds and hearts of all those hundreds and hundreds of students that she inspired in her 96 years.

6

Unforgettable

Andrea Woronick

When you grow up with a brother like Bob, you learn that days don't ever have to be dull. At times we were as close as two peas in a pod and at times so at odds that it was hard to tell that we were brother and sister. He was four when I was born, and yet, he didn't lord it over me. In fact, we spent a lot of time as a duo. And we got in some tight spots, such as when our dad had to pull us out when we were stuck in the toy box or the time we fell in the lake at our grandparents' house.

Bob was a true child of the 60s. He had a van, grew his hair long, took up the guitar, and loved the Beatles. I can still see my mother's face when she got home from the store one day and saw a yellow submarine painted on his bedroom wall. (I think it's still there!)

Bob lived life large — and loved it. If there was a bash, he was there. On one Fourth of July, he set off so many fireworks that the fire department had to be called to put out a fire on a neighbor's roof.

Not much got him mad. His laugh and his shrug let us know that the best way to cope with snags in life was to just let them go. When those near him were stressed out with things, Bob would sit with his eyes closed and his face toward the sun or head for the sea, a fishing rod in hand.

In his late 30s, Bob came down with a rare form of cancer, but with months of radiation and chemo he beat it and then didn't look back. His motto: Life is meant to be lived. Most would have told you all about their meds and what they had to face, but not Bob. When we asked him how he was, he always just said, "'Good. You?"

When Bob reached his 50s, he took up his guitar once more and played night and day. Each time the family was in one room, Bob would strum and sing for us. Some songs were known; some were his own. He would start with some rock-n-roll, move to some sweet Elvis and then right to smooth jazz while singing scat. We loved it when we saw that guitar come out of its case. The best times were when he would visit our mom at the Alzheimer's home and sing and play for her. By her smile, we could tell that she knew he was there.

A few years back, Bob caught a virus that ended up killing most of his heart muscle. He saw lots of doctors, but there wasn't much they could do. Bob had to move to the South for his health, the winters in the Northeast being too harsh for him. I will keep in my heart the last time that he went to see my mom. I can still see him kneeling in front of her singing "Love Me Tender," knowing that this was his last goodbye.

And yet, even though he knew that this illness would take his life — and it did — he kept on with his smiles, jokes, and music. At his end, he had more life in him than most ever do. To all who knew him, Bob was unforgettable. The day he closed his eyes that last time, some of the world's music died with him.

7

Forged in Steel

Ali Larkin Kincaid

On my first day in the chair of Mary Scholz*, I had an open mind. I liked what she did with my friend's hair and felt that what she charged was fair. What's more, it was a good time to make a change since I had been banned from my last salon for being "too critical."

I took my first sight of Mary's shop as a great sign — since it bore none of the chaos of my old salon. That place had been full of kids running all over the vinyl floor while mothers sat in hard chairs — made not from wood but a mold — amid dust in the corners and other grunge in plain view. It took me eons to put out of my mind the time a stylist poured cold permanent solution straight down my back, which soaked the suede vest I wore that day.

When seen in light of that place, Mary's world seems like a high-end B&B. At the front of her home is a large area that we enter from a quaint porch through a Swiss-Alpine door. The room is quiet, often empty, but for Mary. Bathed with sun or — on dim days — with soft lights that come from lamps with rosy shades, all its decor match just so. From the Italian tile floor to the couch, to the rose color that draws all as one — even to the art on the walls — Mary's place can feel like an oasis. Music plays from mixes Mary has pulled from the Big Band era, strains from the likes of Paul Anka and Frank Sinatra, and also classic pop and rock. Some have music only (mostly strings).

But for me, as early as that very first visit, the mood she had shaped shattered fast. After she heard that I washed my hair only every other day, this tall, blond-by-choice aged 60-ish woman glared at me with distaste and said, "All your friends notice, but they're just too nice to tell you." That day, I left her salon on the verge of tears.

This is Mary. There is a price to pay for her great skill with hair, her fair costs, and her eye for decor in her homey shop. Frank and blunt, her words are often harsh as well. The tradeoff for the quiet of her salon can be seen in the wood-burnt sign she has placed on the side of her desk that faces the couch: "Children will remain seated at all times." In just shy of 20 years, I have never seen a child in her place.

When I talked to my friend about ways that Mary's words can sting, my friend told me that her mother had vowed to go to a new salon after Mary told the 75-year-old woman to wipe her feet before she came in.

I had guessed that Mary wouldn't be happy if I were to get there late or, worse yet, not show up at all, but I soon found that Mary isn't happy even when one of us gets there early. Based on her pride in the high bar she sets for her life and work, I think I know why she acts this way. It's only a guess, but I think Mary just doesn't want any of us to have to wait. But we don't tend to see such care as good— at least by the way we feel after she chides us.

When I helped her write her memoir, I saw the way Mary's past had shaped the woman she is today. She lost her father at a young age and not many years later sought to become a nun. Just prior to the last chance to back out of The Order, she saw that this wasn't God's will for her. Later, she wed a German man well past the age that her father would have been. What she kept from the time she trained to be a nun was a strict and rigid view toward life. At any time, she is ready to share what she thinks as if being about to issue an edict. These and other traits are what have caused me to think of her as "The Hair Nazi."

I've watched only clips of the show, *Seinfeld*, but we've all heard of the "Soup Nazi" and how he earned that title. What sealed the title with Mary is when I learned that back in Germany — as a very young man — her much-older husband had once served as one of Hitler's body guards. (It seems that Hitler didn't care if his guards were Nazis, only that they were large and strong!)

The other Mary I came to know from her book bears a depth of trust and faith in God that I have seen in no other. No one — no thing — on earth comes before what she sees as God's will. After she prays, Mary will watch for some sign of where God wants her to go, what He wants her to do. Then, with no turn to the left or the right, she will launch out to do this. Even when it may seem that she is taking a step out on nothing but air, she will trust God to guide her. In every day of her life, she seeks only Him with never any doubt and, as long as she is on this path, every day for her is filled with a sense of peace.

Her strong suit may not be mine, but at times I share her weak one. I, too, can value the pithy word too much and aim it with more fire than tact. I, too, can be rigid in what I think about any area of life. So of course, I cannot cast the first stone.

In fact, as long as I take care in what topic I choose, Mary and I have joined in many deep talks, and more than once in the calm air of her shop, we have bowed our heads in prayer. I value that about Mary. True, she may often act like a "hair Nazi," but I have to admit that I can only hope to one day share the utter strength of her armor of faith.

* not her real name

8

Mervin Evans, Patriot

Dennis Conrad

At six foot three, Mervin Evans was a striking figure. Over 20 times, he ran for political office for the Los Angeles City Council, Controller, and Assessor. He never won. Yet, he fought hard for Veteran's rights, racial equality, and safe streets. His ads are still on YouTube.

To get his name known, Mervin spoke at forums, was a guest on talk radio, and walked door-to-door. He wrote books like *The Issue Book: A Public Policy for a Better California* and sold them on Amazon.com.

I knew Mervin from the speech team at L.A. High School. He was fearless and could speak to a crowd of any size. He did so well that he earned the right to go the state speech contest.

After high school, Mervin joined the United States Army. To help a disabled brother and to put his sister through school, he sent home most of what he earned. Busy in his Armored Calvary unit, he still found time to earn an A.A. degree. Once out of the Army, he spent a year at the University of California, Santa Cruz.

After he came back to L.A., he got a start in politics as an aide with California Assemblywoman Maxine Waters. Then, for 35 years he worked for David Gould, a political consultant. David had also been a part of our high-school speech team.

Early on, David bought Mervin an as-is car from Honest Jim's Car Lot for $500. His goal was to have Mervin put up and take down political signs for him. Here's the rest of the story, as David tells it:

> When Merv started driving after getting gas, the front driver's-side wheel fell off the car. The wheel rolled into a police car that, in turn, ran into a light post. The block

on the car fell down in the middle of the street. Merv was cited for driving an unsafe vehicle on the road.

Months later, Mervin was picked up by police since he fit the profile of a perp in a robbery. Even though cleared of the crime, he was kept in jail since the "unsafe-vehicle" ticket still hadn't been paid. When the judge heard Merv's whole story, he threw out the case and told the police to dismiss the ticket.

After six more months, Mervin was stopped again. This time, it was because the ticket still hadn't been removed by the cops. When Mervin stood in front of the same judge, the judge was mad — but only at the police. Mervin, on the other hand, was free to go.

One time, David asked Mervin to go with him, his father, and a group of Boy Scouts on a Colorado River trip. Mervin had grown up in inner city Los Angeles, so this was going to be new to him. At one point, when the three adults were in the canoe, Mervin and David tried to switch seats. Instead, Mervin tipped over the canoe and David's father ended up under the canoe — along with the scout's lunches.

Even though he had been a lifeguard, Mervin began to shout, "Help! I'm drowning!"

David shouted back, "Just stand up." When Mervin stood up, he found that the water came up only to his knees.

Later, Mervin hatched a money-making idea: to drive people from the airport to a local hotel. Mervin asked David if he could rent a van on David's Visa card and then bring it back a few weeks later.

David agreed, but Mervin kept the van too long. When David's wife, Deborah, saw the bill, she drove to LAX where she walked up to the van, got in, and went with Mervin to take the van back to the car-rental firm.

Some years later, Deborah said to David about Mervin, "When he's old, he'll be living in our garage. Instead of the way you have been paying him for odd jobs, you need to put him on payroll so he'll have Social Security."

Soon David hired him full time with benefits.

Ingrid Orellana, David's partner, shared her Mervin story:

> Mervin and I were in the lobby on the 42nd floor of the downtown office when a man walked in the door. He was the new campaign manager of my client. Without even saying hello, Mervin told him in a deep voice, "She's married. Don't even talk to her. Stay away from her."
>
> The man looked at me. I said, "I'm sorry, you are — ?"
>
> "Demetrius."
>
> Years later, Demetrius became my boyfriend.

Mervin was 62 when he died on January 1, 2016. The night of the viewing, David got to the funeral home early. He saw Mervin in a casket that read "Patriarch," but Mervin didn't have any kids. Before others came to say their goodbyes, David had made sure that the casket said "Patriot."

The next day at Mervin's funeral, a letter from Congresswoman Maxine Waters was read by her daughter. It praised Mervin for his years of hard work. The California State Assembly and the Los Angeles City Council sent framed proclamations that were given to Mervin's sister. On the day of the service, both the city council and the state legislature closed their day in Mervin's honor.

When his friends gather and hear Mervin's name, we always smile and tell "Mervin stories." We miss our amazing friend.

9

Fragile Farewell

Lanita Bradley Boyd

Mother and Daddy were people who "made visits." If a person was sick or there had been a death in the family, Mother and Daddy would be there to help. When they heard that Daddy's old friend, Miss Marie Moore, had gone to live in a nursing home, they went to see her.

When they got there, Daddy stopped a nurse. "We're here to visit Mrs. Moore," he said. "Does she — does she recognize people?"

"Miss Marie?" she asked. He gave a nod. "Not really." The nurse shook her head. "Sometimes we think she does understand even when she doesn't respond. On rare days she seems to know her daughter. It breaks our hearts. You know, lots of us here at the nursing home had her as a teacher at one time or another. She was unique. She was a classy lady, all right." The nurse smiled. "Remember when there wasn't a sharper mind than hers anywhere?"

"Do I know you?" Daddy asked.

"Oh, yes!" She laughed. "I had you for biology years ago. I'm Norma Atkinson." She went on. "Do you notice we still say 'Miss Mah-ree' like she always did? When new girls come in and start calling her 'Mrs. Moore' or even 'Muh-ree,' — can you imagine such disrespect? — we straighten them out right away. We say, 'This is Miss Mah-ree,' who was a childhood friend of Madame Chiang Kai Shek and the best teacher Sumner County High School ever had. You be sure to show her the proper respect. And pronounce her name right!' And they do!"

My parents smiled then moved down the hall to Miss Marie's room.

The elegant white head rested lightly on the fresh pillow. They stood at each side of the bed.

"Miss Marie, it's Lawrence," he said. "Mary and I came by to say hello. You have a nice neat place here."

The old eyelids fluttered slightly. She stared blankly at each of them in turn with no sign that she knew them.

Daddy spoke at length of days past — of the high school where they had taught, of students and teachers they had known, of news since they'd both left — she to retire, he for another school.

"You and I used to sing some pretty good duets at those school talent shows, didn't we? We don't even hear most of those old songs anymore, but everyone loved them back then. Remember 'The Rose of Tralee' and 'Silver Threads Among the Gold'? And how about 'I'll Take You Home Again, Kathleen'? Your voice was fantastic. I still think of you when I hear a clear, melodic voice that can really master those high notes."

He looked to Mother for some help to reach his friend. "Our children

are all doing well, Miss Marie," she said. "They all loved having you in school. You know, that last year you taught, Lanita changed her whole four-year plan of courses so she could take as many classes as possible from you. You're just about a saint to everybody you ever taught."

Daddy began again. "All of us who had grown up in the country and had never been very sophisticated were glad that we could sit at your feet. You knew something about everything. We'd never had a teacher that could teach Latin and English literature and algebra equally well. You had such style, such verve, about everything you ever did. You taught us to respect God and each other. You taught us all that *what* we do in life is not more important than *how* we do it."

"I guess we'll be going now," Daddy said. "I don't know if you understood any of this or not. They were things I should have said to you long ago and never did. You were such a great influence on my life when you were my teacher, and then even more when we taught together. You made me understand about teenagers and caring.

"Until we had all those long conversations about students and teaching, I had never had a glimmer of understanding as to why you were so successful with every student — no matter what their backgrounds or needs. You taught me that demanding only the best from each of them was the greatest way to show them how much you cared. You were always my role model, and I felt like I had to come and tell you so. Any success I have had as a teacher I owe to you.

"I hope you understood some of this." He paused, watching for some response. "Good-bye, now."

Hand in hand, Daddy and Mother walked toward the door, loathe to leave. Then they were stopped by a gentle quavering sound. "Dah-ling, I am grow-ing o-old. Sil-ver threads among the gold," the aged voice sang. Daddy was instantly at her side, his gentle tenor joining her wispy soprano. "Shine upon my brow to-da-ay; life is fading fast a-way."

"But, my dah-ling, you will be-e-e, Al-ways young and fair to me. Yes, my dah-ling, you will be-e, Always young and fair to me."

Her voice gained strength and her enunciation was flawless as Daddy grasped the fragile hand. "Dah-ling, I am growing o-old, Silver threads among the gold. Shine upon my brow today; Life is fading fast away."

Miss Marie smiled, her eyes now closed. Her strength was drained, but her face showed both joy and peace. Her student, her mentee, her friend, had come to pay tribute, and she had come through, as always, with style.

10

The Man of Adventure

Cristina Moore

John climbs tall peaks, dives in all the oceans, and flies above the earth. He has danced with Indonesian kids, kissed an eel, and run from apes. He eats all that is placed in front of him — "no questions asked." He finds joy in all that breathes and all that God has made.

Our lives crossed on a dive trip to Galapagos. In his past life, John had a job and a home but no spouse or child. These days, he doesn't work and has no home. Now in his 60s, he has the get-up-and-go of a man in his 30s. He has no fear and lives for his trips. He has cash to burn and life to live. He strives to touch and see it all. Of his view toward life he says, "I have only so many matches left in the box to strike, so I'm trying to make sure they all light and burn brightly."

John loves to hike, bike, dive, jump, and climb. He leaves no rock in place and takes pics along the way to share his joy. His heart soars when his trips stir others to go live their lives to the full. His age is not who he is; his taste for life is what makes him.

Although John has no home, now and then he needs a place to rest his head. This place to rest is our home. For the last four years, John has stayed with us in November and December. Our girls call him "Uncle John" and look forward to his visits. He loves to hear my girls laugh, and the noise of our home. We all laugh, talk, and enjoy day-to-day tasks. We eat and drink, and he shares tales of his trips with our girls and their friends. At the end of December, John always leaves for his next big adventure with a wave and a hug.

I am glad for the chance trip that brought us John and can't wait for next November!

11

Being Jackie

Pam Groupe Groves

At lunch on my folk's patio we laughed and cried at the shared family stories. My mom told a 70-year-old story that was new to the third generation in the group. "When your Aunt Jackie and I were ten and eight, I would often be blocks away from home when night came on. Mom would send Jackie to bring me home. She brought me home but not the way mom thought she would. Jackie would march me down the street with her rifle at my back." Jackie's strong voice broke into the story, "It wasn't my rifle, it was my BB gun, and it only happened once!" My sister and I looked at each other in quiet shock. It was the first time Aunt Jackie had agreed that a march down the street by gunpoint did occur. We then burst into a laugh fest fueled by the thought: *Did Jackie actually think it was okay because it was only a BB gun and it was a one-time event?*

Jackie on the right with Pam's mom, Betty Jo.

For sure we were aware that as an adult Aunt Jackie chose her own way to live. The BB gun story showed that choosing her own way had begun early in her life.

Aunt Jackie told me once, "I knew in high school I needed an uncomplicated life, a simple life. I needed a life where I had only myself to be responsible for." I thought this was a rare sense of self for a young teen who grew up in an era in which the "society rule" for a girl was to grow up, graduate from high school, marry, have kids, and put her family first.

Her older sister did just that. The family had not talked about other life roles that daughters could choose.

One day, in her last year of high school, Jackie ran into a friend who was taking the trolley to visit Marylhurst College. Jackie tagged along. That day Jackie found out what she would do next in life. She would be the first in her family to go to college.

When the money she had saved from her high school job as a waitress ran out, she found a way to put college on hold and go back later. She joined the Air Force with the long-term goal to have funds to pay for school.

I was four when her life in the Air Force began; I found out years later that Jackie had been sent to the Strategic Air Command office. General Curtis LeMay felt that her math and clerical skills would be a great asset. She worked at SAC until she was on to her next life goal, going to Oregon State College.

After college, she began her life's work in jobs using her math skills. She told me many times, "Work is to pay for food and housing. Off-time is to do what you love." Off-work is where the real Jackie lived. She went fishing, hiking, worked in the yard, and added to the lives of her nieces and nephews. She found her sweet place when she bought an old farm house on 15 acres with a creek at the edge of her land.

When she wasn't at work, Aunt Jackie dressed in her own way. First choice on a hot day was her best vivid red top with orange plaid shorts. When she saw that a pair of slacks she was wearing had a small hole, she fixed it with a tiny safety pin. She liked the look so much that she added eight more pins of varied sizes and wore the slacks often. A garb I still see in my mind's eye is a color-filled Christmas tree skirt that she wore as a shawl to our family Christmas party and the Christmas event at church.

In Aunt Jackie's final days of life, I heard a nurse say to her, "I see you were in the Air Force 60 years ago. What did you do?" In a firm voice Jackie said, "Oh, I can't talk about that. I did top security clearance work for General LeMay." This was a new angle. I'd never heard this part of her Air Force story. In my mind, hers had been dull office tasks. With this new idea I mused: *Who would think they couldn't say a word about their military work after 60 years had passed? I guess that was Jackie being Jackie.*

A few years later, the classified Air Force base in Nevada called Area 51 was once again in the news. My thoughts went back to Aunt Jackie's lack of words about her work at the SAC office. It hit me that I couldn't recall her ever saying a word about Area 51. She hadn't talked about it when it was in the news or even when we drove through the area on a road trip. She didn't speak of it in 2005 when the CIA did admit, for the first time, that Area 51 did exist and also declassified some files. I was once again awe-struck by Aunt Jackie. She chose to hold firm and not talk about her SAC work. She could have "wowed" many with her story. To keep quiet was not what most would have done, but that was Jackie.

Seeing Aunt Jackie live in her own way taught me a truth that I value to this day: It is okay to have a life that strays from the norm.

"Thank you, Aunt Jackie."

Jackie being lifted by friends.

12

GWTF

Julie Ann Chase

The first time I went to her church I was keen to know who this "Ruth" was. Folks spoke of her with such love, and I was ready for a change. At first, I could not see her. Slight and short with soft gray hair, she was like a flat black-and-white photo until she began to dart back and forth in the front of the room with cheer, her hands out to all there, eyes quick and eager to greet new ones like me. As she moved and spoke, I both saw and felt her depth of love, much like a prism of light. Her broad smile was full of teeth and as wide as her face. That smile set her apart. Like a small house wren, she would flit, and her laugh had a clear song to it that all could hear. In her "nest" were more smiles and laughs — such as I had never seen in church. What a new way to meet with God!

The church bells rang, and she led us with zeal. She made me feel at ease and calm. A woman at the helm was also a novel sight for my eyes.

What Ruth brought was new for me, and it took me off guard. She gave a sense that all of us were equal. In place of heavy dogma, she brought such joy! At one point she said, "You are where you want to be," and it was true. And then out came her wide grin, yet again! All I heard in her voice was pure love. It was as if I had watched her click her heels and say, "There's no place like home," and it was true. I was home.

Over the years, her words of faith were a balm to my soul. I was drawn to hear her. The way her eyes would seek each of us out helped me to feel Him by my side. Her voice made me hang onto her words, and when I would tell her what was on my heart she gave her whole self to hear me. She did this for all, with a smile — a gift she learned from her time spent with Mother Theresa who told her, "Peace begins with a smile."

Ruth hears with her eyes and sees what is not said. She speaks her faith by true acts of love, not just words. "GWTF" she says often . . . "Go With the Flow." Her eyes light up like a child when she says GWTF, as if each new turn of fate could bring a game to win. And games, well, watch out — she likes to win! When I close my eyes and see her face, it shows joy. It shows light. It is love.

The whole time Ruth was at our church I was like a small chick who would reach for her words to feed my heart and soul. Each week I was filled, and her songs are still vivid in my mind. This small, slight bird of love gave wings to my heart. And the nest she built gave me a new life. I found out what it meant to go with the flow. It meant to feel spunk and fun as I learned to fly with Him.

13

Friday Night Lights

Becky Alexander

For four years I never missed a high school football game, but I don't think I ever watched one. Football games weren't about football. They were about kids clad in red and white with short skirts and white boots with red pom poms. They were about cold Ohio nights, quilts to stay warm, and hot cocoa from the snack stand. And football games were most of all about the halftime show.

As part of the drill team in the Mohawk marching band, I took the field each Friday night with 15 friends. We danced to "S-A-T-U-R-D-A-Y Night," "The Rockford Files," and "Do the Hustle." Most of the time, we used shakers for our routines. That worked great for me, as I could hold one in my prosthetic left hand. I'd dance in front of the porch panes of my house and watch my image to make sure the moves with my left arm looked the same as the moves with my right. All was well until the red and white gloves.

Beth, our captain, said that we would wear cool gloves for our next routine. She pulled a pair from her purse and put them on. They were white on the back and red on the palm. "At some points in the routine, we will flash all white," Beth said. "At other points, we will flash all red."

When Beth showed us some moves, my heart sank. I knew I couldn't do that. My prosthetic hand would only open and close; it wouldn't turn at the wrist, and the fingers wouldn't stretch out straight.

Later that day I talked with Dad. "For the first time, I'm going to have to sit out a game," I told him.

He scrunched his brow and said, "Don't give up just yet. Let me think about it."

That night Dad went to work at Armco Steel. He shared my story with the other machinists on his shift. They used their break time to offer ideas. As they talked of the need for the wrist to turn, a man named Gene asked, "What about an ice cream scoop? You know the kind that you push the lever and the piece slides along the inner side of the scoop? What if we could find a way to use those parts that turn?"

Dad and all the guys grew quiet. "You could be on the right track there, Gene," Dad said.

"I've got one at home," Gene added. "I'll bring it to work for us to look at."

The next day Dad and his friends hooked the parts from the ice cream scoop to my prosthetic wrist and cable. They made straight "fingers" from strips of metal, put pads on them, and pulled the red and white glove over them. The "hand" looked like a real hand! The cable that once made my hand open and close now turned it from red to white!

I don't know if the Mohawks won the football game that Friday night. I can't name the quarterback or the Most Valuable Player. But of one thing I am very sure; my dad was the star of the game.

14

To Merit an "A"

Cybele Sieradzki

Elizabeth Hope Jackson, Ph.D., never gave up on me. Professor of English at Maryville College in East Tennessee, she gave five grades on every paper we wrote. She turned my first paper face down when she gave it back.

I turned it over. Three "A's," one "B," and an "F." I'd never gotten an "F" in my life. Next to the "F," she wrote the word, "Plagiarism," a word I had not seen.

"I don't know what this word means," I said to Dr. Jackson.

"You did not use the right notes."

"But I did use footnotes." She said I had not used them to show where I'd used whole ideas as well as quotes. Then she asked where I'd gone to high school.

I named the tiny school deep in Appalachia. "I never wrote a paper," I told her. "I'm not ready for your Advanced English class, even though I passed the test for it."

"I can see that. But I can also see that you are bright. I'll keep you in the class if you will work hard."

We both worked hard. We met after class more often than not. I wrote, changed, and wrote again. I learned the rules. While in her class, I often was not on time and my work was always a day late.

"Why?" Dr. Jackson asked.

"I don't know." Truly, I didn't know then, but I know now. I felt I didn't merit an "A" from her.

For three more years, I took every class she taught. Each time, on my late paper, she crossed out the grade "A," and changed it to a "B."

She'd shake her head and frown, but never once did she even hint that we were done or that I should not become a writer. Years later, when I wrote for jobs and won praise, I gave thanks for Dr. Jackson and, most of all, her faith in me.

We all found joy in each class Dr. Jackson taught. Her bright eyes peered across her tall desk and dared our thoughts to be more honed. She taught with élan, with well-learned depth and breadth of each topic. With glee, she danced back and forth among the front row of desks.

In class, we would watch her famed small stack of notes. She wrote on tiny scraps the size of stamps, torn from who knew where — cards, notebooks, check stubs, bills, and menus. While she talked, she slid the notes in her hands up and down in the stack. Her hands never stopped their task, even though she might look at only the top note once or twice.

She peered into the veiled realm of her topic and spoke with a soft, yet firm, voice that said more than the mere words she shared. Best of all, she had a good sense of play and a fine way of fun; she loved to end with a pun.

15

Four Peas in a Pod

Liz Kimmel

Ben and Hannah, friends of mine from church, have four kids whose ages range from four to twelve. The crazy things they say can crack a smile from even the most stern-faced among us.

Norah, the one with the least time here on earth, holds her own with the older kids. "I have a real fun game we could play. It's called, 'Take out your eye-balls and put them in the trash.' "

One day, after she put her pants on with the back in the front, Norah looked down in awe and yelled, "Hey! New pockets!"

The four most scary words one may ever hear are, "Where did Norah go?" Case in point, this chat with her mom:

Norah: "Need a knife."

Mom: "Why?"

Norah: "Saw a yucky bug."

Next going up the line is Wesley. When he was only two he told a friend, "When you run away from Mommy you smack your face into walls." That makes sense.

Wes asks lots of things of his mom and dad, like . . .

"Mom, do I have stripes? . . . I feel like I have stripes."

"Why haven't you taken my baby out yet?!" (It was hard to wait for Norah to get here.)

"What's that sound? . . . It smells like Mickey Mouse."

He also has sweet things to say. "Mom, this is mine, but it's yours now. I love you." And then he gave her his used tooth floss. Once he told her, "Mom, don't break my heart, and I won't break your heart."

One day Hannah had to tell Wesley some very vital news. "Are you all ears?" Wesley, in a very blasé tone of voice said, "No, I never am."

While on the road one day Wes piped up from the back seat:

Wes: "Are we low on gas?"

Mom: "No. The tank is full."

Wes: "Then why are you going so slow?"

Big sister Sage did not like to wait, either. One day Hannah said, "Sage, you may watch My Little Pony when I am done with my mocha. With the rough voice of a drill sergeant her daughter cried, "Drink it! Drink it! Drink it! Drink it! Drink it! Drink it! Drink it!"

Never mind, thought Hannah, her bit of peace gone in a flash.

With two boys in the house, both Sage and Hannah knew that any sense of peace would be rare. The kids played; the kids fought. In any clash, the boys would come out on top. Once, as Sage raced up the stairs, Hannah asked why. Sage: "I'm going to get my knife!"

One day, when play was done and it was time to eat, this was heard between mom and girl:

Mom: "Did you wash your hands?

Sage: "Yes. Do you trust me on that? Please trust me on that."

Sage learned to be both sweet and silly from Cooper, the first-born child. One day, during nap time, four-year-old Cooper kept two-year old Sage awake. But it was hard for his folks to yell at him, since what they heard again and again was, "Sage! Hey Sage! I love you!"

Even at a young age, Cooper was very aware of how those near him looked. One day at the store, amid non-stop talk about all that he saw, he paused and dropped these words on his mom: "You look great right now, by the way." Hannah asked him to say that again, just to be sure that she'd heard him right. She had. *Watch out, girls! He's got charm.*

On the other hand was the time he told her, "Mom, can I get a comb for your hair? It looks . . . funky." And the day when he said, "Mom, I like your hair today! You look like Jimmy Neutron!"

Cooper wasn't always thrilled with his folks. After being sent to do a task he said, "I'm gonna be more tall than you when I'm grown up.

You'll have to look up at me when you tell me what to do."

The kids were taught at home this year, and part of Cooper's daily work was to write out the spelling words of the week for his mom to check. But most of them were spelled wrong, which caused Hannah to scratch her head — since Cooper spells very well. Then she glanced over at him and saw that he was bent over, not able to keep his mirth under wraps any more. "Got ya, mom!"

These four cool and crazy kids form quite a team. One night, when Norah was just a baby, the other three came down from their rooms, one at a time, to ask if all was well in the house. Hannah told them it was and sent each one back to his bed. When it was Wesley's turn to come down and check with Mom, he cleared it all up for her. "We made a deal today. If there is any threat, Cooper will fight for all of us. If he dies, Sage will fight for all of us. If she dies, I will fight! We just want to make sure you're okay." They were all glad at her reply, but also bummed that they didn't have to fight.

If each of these four kids have brimmed with this much originality at such a young age, what will they be like when they grow up?

For them and those around them, life will never be dull.

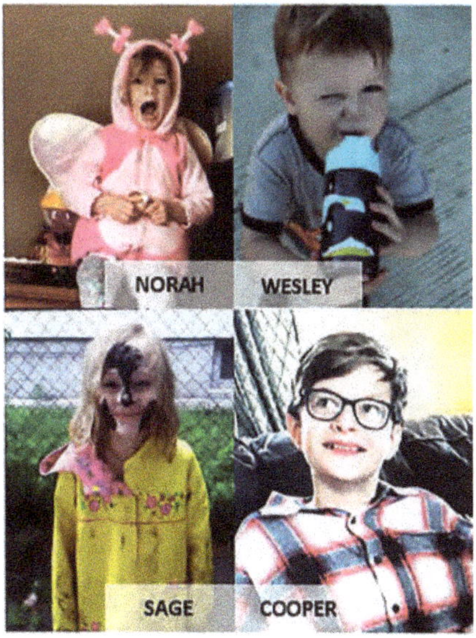

16

A Rare Gift

Penny L. Hunt

Acres of short, green, peach trees held no thrill for me when we moved west from the low-country coast of South Carolina to the tiny town of Trenton. Barbecues were a far cry from shrimp boils; and bass ponds made me long for sea, salt, and the beach.

While still sad and new in town, I was asked to come to a Southern Living party at a Miss South Carolina's home.

What on earth would I wear?

Once there, I was not sure why guests used the side door of the house and not the grand front entry with its huge wreath and pots of ferns. I made my way in with some other guests and for the first time saw Jane Jenkins Herlong — queen bee of the town and past Miss South Carolina. She had pulled her blue shirt up to her chin to show off her new Body Spanx. Right then, I knew we would be friends.

As the night came to an end, the idea to book a Southern Living party of our own was put forth as a way to help Jane earn a pie-pan gift. A laugh came from all sides of the room. The guest next to me slapped her knee and said, "Well, that thing won't ever see the light of day." *How rude!* I didn't get why she'd say such a thing until later when Jane made a dish with grits, and I told her how much I liked it. She made me swear not to tell a soul. "It will ruin my image."

As I came to know Jane over the years, she became more and more of a force in my life. When my hip was down to bone on bone and I had to have a new one put in, Jane drove me to the mall to buy the things I'd need.

That day I was in so much pain I couldn't walk, so she got me a chair with wheels, and we were off! All went well until we came to the aisle with bras. The chair was too wide for the over-packed rows, and we ended up with a trail of clothes as long as a kite's tail.

The span of sizes, styles, and colors of the things we had in tow was vast. We tried to put them back in their right spots but were not doing well when a man with a badge came to see what we were up to. The chair was now stuck on the leg of a table and would not budge. Badge Man was not at all happy when he had to lift the chair to set me free. I kept saying, "Sorry," and was near tears when Jane saved the day.

With every bit of her Miss South Carolina charm she said in fluty tones, "Oh, thank you so much. You are too kind. I don't know *what* I would have done if a man as strong as you had not come to help us." He lapped that up as if it were honey, and we were not run out of the store.

By then, I didn't want to do much more than go home. But we made one last stop at the mall café where Jane gave me a drink called Cardiac Arrest. "Drink up," she said, "This will be good for you. It'll either pep you up or kill you, and then that'll be the end of it." I drank it, lived, and we laughed all the way home.

Jane's car is a huge SUV — more a dress rack on wheels, with shoes and bags to match them on all the seats. Her mama used to call it "The

Bus." We've had lots of long talks and shared tears in that thing, but no matter what, Jane finds a way to end each trip with a smile.

Once, on our way to a National Speakers Association event, I was a mass of nerves. Jane drove up to a Dairy Queen, jumped out, and came back with two huge Peanut Buster Parfaits. "Don't worry," she said. We'll skip the salad bar." When later, on the trip, The Bus hit a deer, Jane used a roll of duct tape to strap the front of the car back in place and a black Sharpie to draw the grill. "No one will notice," she said. "It's the same color as the car."

Other days with Jane have been spent far from our small town on the farm where she grew up on Johns Island. The low-country home she knew as a child sits near a creek where live oaks shade a long, lush lawn. On the porch hang two signs. One reads: "Not everyone can be queen. Someone has to stand on the curb and wave as I go by." The other reads: "*As for me and my household, we will serve the Lord.* Joshua 24:14." Both are true and I love her for it.

"Mi casa su casa" has been Jane's way of life since the day I met her, and when my granddaughter was to be wed, the farm was a shoo-in as the best venue. When a six-foot alligator was spied near one of the tents Jane said, "Now, don't you worry, Sugar. That gator won't bother you if you don't bother him. Just don't try and feed him."

She'll pass two Starbucks in search of a McDonald's latte, hold a Valentine's Day party at Waffle House, fill the back yard with folks to watch the moon cover the sun, and make us all laugh till we cry with her, "southern fried humor and sweet tea wisdom."

I still miss the coast but would not trade the rare gift God has given me in my Miss South Carolina friend — for all the salt in the sea.

17

Romeo Papa One

Jorja Davis

Romeo Papa One requesting permission for take-off on runway two niner." That was my daddy's dream.

When I was young, the flight was earth bound — just his land kite, which is what he called his motorcycle — and a home-built go-cart. What a thrill of joy was ours as we flew on the go-cart! I learned the hard way about turns and rocks. Do you know how hard it is to flip a go-cart? He would smile as he helped me back on. "Anything worth doing," he said, "should make you a little bit afraid."

I think about the motor-oil smell of his auto shop at the high school. There on the wall hung the poem "High Flight," by John Gillespie Magee that begins, "Oh, I have slipped the surly bonds of earth/And danced the skies on laughter-silvered wings" and ends: "Put out my hand and touched the face of God."

When he moved to the new high school, the poem moved with him. It then moved to his small study space the year he lived 500 miles from home to wrap-up his PhD. That year I turned 16. Even the note he wrote me was filled with thoughts of flight: "as your experience with 16 is limited, so is ours as we have never been the parents of a 16-year-old before. We stand on the runway together . . . . You are in the pilot's seat . . . . Do you wish clearance for takeoff? Remember, anything worth doing should make you a little bit afraid."

When I was grown, "High Flight" moved again. But with it hung a tail-less shirt torn by his flight instructor the day he came back from his first solo flight. Then my father bought a one-prop, two-seat plane. To take my mind off Vietnam on the day my husband left for boot camp,

Daddy took me for my first flight.

When I felt the lift of the wheels, I turned my eyes from the blur of grass to the trees and phone wires ahead. My eyes now closed, I heard his whoop as we rose into the air. I dragged my eyes open to ask to go home, but the look of joy on his face caused me to bite my lip and renew my grip on the arm rests.

We stood on wing tip to fly 'round my in-law's house and zoomed low over the trees. As we banked away, a black wall of rain heaved into sight. "We'll have to head back," he said, as the first gust rocked the piece of metal that held us in the sky. When we reached the grass strip, he chose to make the dog-leg again to get more of a feel for the cross wind.

"Full throttle and no flaps," he said as we began to land. The gusto in his eyes gave lie to his sober voice. This was what he lived for, to come in so fast that no room was left for error. As the grass swooped up, I held my breath — my hands numb.

What he saw in my pale face was awe. My real thoughts came clear when he helped me out; my knees gave way. "Anything worth doing," he said, "should make you a little bit afraid."

He longed for a plane with hook-on wings, a plane he could pull behind his land kite. "High Flight" had found its place on the wall among tools and plans. He began to build the Bede 5. The body of the plane was the size of a bathtub. The wings were too long to hook on in the one-car garage he had turned into a shop. The wings hung next to the flight suit tagged with the plane's call sign — "Romeo Papa One."

To sate his need to log the time he spent to create the Bede 5, he altered his radio. While it tracked the time he spent fine-tuning the drill press to get the least amount of dip in the rivet holes, it also made his heart soar and bank to Tchaikovsky. While he wrote a piece for *Sport Aviation – The Experimental Aircraft Magazine* about the best way to sew the cloth for the body and wings, Bach soared along.

The Bede 5 came in sheets of metal and in boxes of this and that. In them were thousands of clecoes in three sizes. It must have taken over 500 of those spring-loaded short-term rivets to clasp the body alone. At this point, the body of the plane looked like the union of a soap-box-derby car and a hedgehog.

Then, before the last rivet went in, came the word from the doctor: Stage 4 Non-Hodgkin's Lymphoma and myocardial infarction. The one sapped his strength; the other clipped his wings.

But he never seemed to grieve. He would stand in his shop to renew himself with the sight of sheet metal and rivets and stay long enough to read "High Flight." Then he sought out his balsa and nylon to build a model of an old-time plane he could fly with a hand-held radio unit. He put his radio, extra tubes, fuel, and a few tools into his home-built cart then drove to an empty lot. There, he turned the cart into a stool and sat to watch his plane dance and dip in the sun.

Three weeks before he died, he penned his own "High Flight."

Sometimes when I reach to touch the hand of God,
I find I'm not quite tall enough, strong enough, unable to locate.
However, if my hand remains outstretched, He seems always
Tall enough, strong enough, and insightful enough to be able to reach me.

The last time I stood by his bed, wracked with all I could not put into words, I asked, "Daddy, aren't you scared to die?" He piled up his strength, drew me close, grinned, and spoke so low I could just about hear: "Anything worth doing should make you a little bit afraid."

"Romeo Papa One, you are cleared for take-off on runway two-niner."

18

Angel Unaware

Susanna Shutz Robar

Today, her name doesn't come to mind. And she had told me only the first name, never the last. She seemed about 20 years old, while I was near 40. Her light-brown hair fell just past the nape of her neck. She was not too tall and had a round shape about her. Her clothes were well-made, in a straight style. With a grin from ear to ear, she spoke a bright "Hi!" to all. I first saw her at a lady's weekend-away. I was part of a team of two, chosen to plan out the three days.

When she came into the lobby of the lodge, I could see in her hand paper shapes in lots of spring colors. When I saw that she was on a search to stick an Easter-theme shape onto each lady's name badge, I thought, *Wait! This is MY event! That is MY name badge!* In her deed, I saw fault, a breach of sorts. My proud heart was harsh, with not even one slice of grace.

After she put Easter shapes on badge after badge, I saw her speak to the wife of our pastor. I was so sure that Marcia would shut down the young woman's plan. But to my great alarm and shock, Marcia gave her a big smile and let the shape of a yellow baby chick get stuck on her name badge. She even said, "Thank you." I could not take it all in. In the vexed part of my heart, I thought I would burst as I tried to keep quiet.

For the rest of the hours of that three-day-event, I made it a point to dodge the young woman at every turn. I feared that if I let her put a silly Easter thing on my name badge, I would also look silly or inane or seem to have no sense. In those days, I would have rather died than look silly or worse.

My many acts to hide from the young woman bore fruit. I was safe

— at least until the final hour of the final day. As I took my last bite of lunch, I saw her through the front glass door of the lunch hall. "You are the hardest person to track down of anyone I know!" she said. "I want to give you an Easter bunny for your name badge!" With her words came that big smile. I could hear my mouth say a small, "Ok" to the bunny stuck on my name badge, while at the same time I could feel my heart shout out, "NO!" But, as she stuck the shape on my badge, she just as quickly took it off with the words, "No. God says that He wants you to have a purple heart." As she put the new shape on my badge, my own heart began to melt into the soft air of God's love.

This young woman then held my hands in hers, took sight of my eyes full of tears, and said, "God wants you to know that He sees your heart, and knows its many wounds, that He sees your places of hurt. He knows every war you have fought in the past and the fight you face today. God wants to tell you that He has never lost sight of you and that He has been with you every step of the way. He sees where you have gone, and He knows where you are going. He knows that life has not been fair to you. But He has good in mind for you, for you are a victorious soldier in God's army. And, so, He wants you to take hold of this purple heart."

In a flash, in her string of words, God took away my hard heart and gave me a soft heart that was more like His. My life began on a new path.

The old need for me to whine, moan, and nag, the one-time quest to judge, rate, and rank — those thoughts blew away and left a light breeze of rest and calm. True, at times I'm still given a push from a dark, far-off place to go back to dead ways. But when that old voice comes to hover by my ears, the still, small voice of God beings me back and I perch on His hand of grace to deny the old pride.

I will never let this young woman's life slip from my mind or from my heart, as I am full of thanks to her for her strong sense of duty to God in His will to set my heart free from a pit of gloom. In the end, this young woman (with not even a first name still in my mind) has the joy of being an angel sent to me by God.

19

The Haitian Sensation

Kenneth Avon White

Dust-bowl-hot was the air, and kicky pop music had the house on fire. It was July, 1988. One week prior, my friend Josh had said, "You gotta meet this guy, Leslie. His old man owns a phat piece of Haiti! 'dude's gonna be huge." In 1988, we'd all set our sights on the rise to a celeb's rank. I thought, *If he's gonna blow up, what could that mean for me?*

The years to come taught me that if I were to lasso a comet, it would come with more ease than to keep up with Leslie Dalencour.

But back then, I didn't know what I know now. Back on that night, down the stairs Josh and I crept. Walls quaked to the beat of funky music. The voice in full swell was radio ready. Leslie was in the thick of prep for a dance-club show — his troupe a team of acne-plagued teens who should have been home doing school work.

On the last step, I stood dead in my tracks. All this was a far cry from my world of film and plays. On the one hand, I watched the teens — with their skill and drive — dart through the room as if they had been shot out of a Barnum and Bailey cannon. On the other hand, I didn't see how this tribe of whelps would be ready in two days for the big show at Washington D.C.'s mega-hip night spot — The Bank on F Street.

And there, in the midst of them was Leslie. Long strings of braids swung back and forth from his head like those huge cloth strands in a car wash. Eyes as big as river stones shot stares right through every young man in the dance troupe. "Stop" Leslie roared. "First you gonna give me this." He busts a move they must have missed. "Then you gonna give me this." Then with a flick of his hand, the tech guy flipped a switch. They would blast off again. At song's end, shouts of praise made it seem as if we'd "gone to church" and back again.

I chimed in with my own praise. "I'm Ken, Josh's friend. That was off the charts!" With a glance that would make Garbo blush, Leslie's words slid from the back of his throat: "It's what I do." If his ego had legs, it would have been ready to run a sprint.

One hour later, he was thrown out of the house he rented from Cleo — the girl he'd once dated. Boots, clothes, gear, and pans were tossed out the door in heaps. Girl dumps boy. Boy lands in the streets.

The look of things didn't add up. But I was hooked — as it seemed were others. We packed Leslie's life into the trunk of my car. The rest of the gang formed a trail from front door to car. It was as if the Pied Piper had leaped from the page of a child's book. In a trance, we sped off toward the home of a fan ready to take him in.

Later at The Bank, I felt as if I'd crawled through the TV screen and onto the stage of the MTV Awards. My work to promote the group had packed this top night spot. Then the teens and the pop king who had shined them up did the rest. This hit led to more shows, like at the grand Palladium. Crowds grew — a mix of fans and those who like to rail about things that change, like when Leslie's braids got swapped out for spikes and vivid greens and pinks and blues. The black garb made of hides was swapped out for a bold clash of color, style, and quasi taste. Leslie called it "free to be." "You're dealt one life. You got to please *you.* That's one," he would say. "Live life for you and do some good along the way. That's two." So many people toed the line. Leslie drew a new line and wooed you to cross over with him.

I did see Leslie "do good along the way." He was a father to kids on the block who had none. When food was scarce, he piled their plates high with slap-your-mamma pasta. When having a car was only a dream, he took the squirts on trips to the beach. Later, I was there when Miami Haitian kids got their visit, along with boxes of goods that Leslie had bought with his own money. It was as if Santa Claus had shown up, minus belly and beard and in an old rusty U-Haul sleigh. Ego and pomp blared from one side of the Leslie Dalencour "coin." Care for those in need shone from the other. Too few can switch from one side to the next with such grace. It takes a spine hard as nails, a soul soft as silk, and a heart that beats for dreams to rise.

Too soon, things got lean. The live shows didn't pay much. Leslie had to work other jobs to keep gas in the car. I urged him to take on Miami where the music scene was red hot. And so, in March of 1991 he moved down on my dime. I was soon paid back — but only in sheer glee — when Leslie dug into his bag of tricks to form a new act out of thin air. In August of 1991, from the streets of Miami Beach, Leslie plucked six Latin teens with beach jobs and morphed them into the boy band *Axis.* The show prep took place in a beach park with a small stage shaped like The Hollywood Bowl. In heat that would nuke a hot dog, Leslie worked those boys like dogs. The boom box blared. The beach goers stared. And in the end, the girls went gaga at Disney World's Treasure Island show — and so did the boys with the big bucks at Sony Music. *Axis* got a music deal, and I flew home with the thought that all was good. But all was not good. *Axis* tried a coup to oust Leslie from the scene. When Leslie called Sony legal to let them know that half the boys couldn't sing and that his voice picked up all the slack, the deal died faster than the Ford Edsel. The boys went back to jobs that paid seven bucks an hour. Leslie went back to a car that had to run on fumes.

In the spring of 1992, Leslie rose from the ashes again — this time out of his ties to Haiti. Haitian music stars wield power in the body politic. So in Haiti, Leslie teamed up with Fedia Laguerre. Known as the Haitian Joan Baez, Fedia's were the songs that made Haitians rise up and oust Duvalier. After death threats and a life in exile in Miami, Fedia's music had waned. Leslie was out to turn gloom into gold for both of them. His plan was to gather Haiti's music elite in a unity gala. Leslie and Fedia would star. The idea was good but with long odds. So Leslie called the Haitian Embassy. The embassy, in turn, called the icons who were at odds with their rivals. Each would soon board a plane for Miami. Then Leslie worked his magic to get a date at Miami's huge James L. Knight Center — with no money down. He made Haitian biz execs step up. I got pegged to help Leslie weave the chaos into an event. So, in April of 1992, I hopped a plane again. It was two days of pure hell on earth . . . and the best two days of my life.

They sent the music stars back home to make right what was wrong. The next day, the paper read: "Haitian Sensation Unites Haiti's Music World." The name has stuck to this day. The event set Leslie up with coups of his own. He was given his own Miami TV talk show and snagged green-room time with mega stars The Fugees – the band that launched Lauryn Hill and Wycliff Jean — and a one-on-one with famed god of the Latin art world, Romero Britto.

From pop king to peace envoy to TV talk-show host — that was Leslie Dalencour's trip through the cosmos! Those years were a wonder to me — a time when we stood the world on its feet, a time when magic was in the air, freeing us to "just be."

20

The IBM Girl

Mary Alice Archer

"Golly. I'm so excited about the possibility of a job and such an exciting one. It sounds like fun. Oh, I do so hope I can get it!" (Martha Smith's Diary, April 1, 1941)

Martha did get the job and became one of the first "IBM Girls," to be trained as a Systems Service Technician.

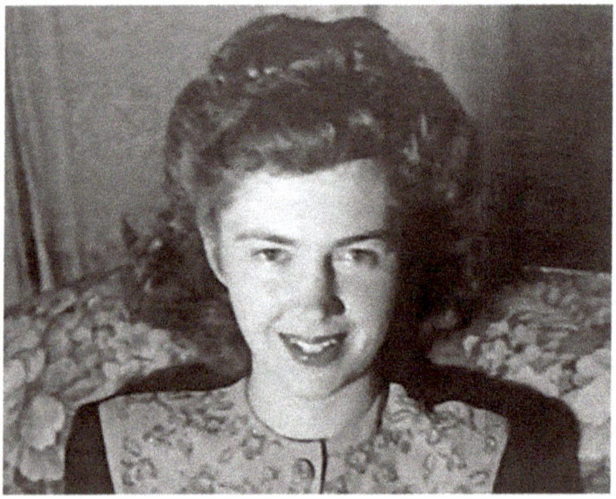

Martha Janney Smith was born in 1918 to Dr. and Mrs. F. Janney Smith. Her father had just been hired to work at the brand-new Henry Ford Hospital in Detroit so Martha led the rare life of private schools, boat-club galas, and shows of all the new films. She even danced the Two-Step with Henry Ford at one of his "country" dances.

Martha loved her time at Sweet Briar Women's College — even when the cows got into the onion patch which gave the milk in the dining hall a strange taste. But after a trip to see a close friend in L.A., Martha asked her father if she could move to the University of Southern California for her last school year. This was the first time she had gone to a co-ed school. In 1940, Martha left with a degree in psychology and a minor in math — a rare feat for a woman at that time.

IBM took great care when they chose sales and service people to teach customers how to use and maintain their brand-new product — business computers. Martha went through more than a month of interviews prior to being hired and sent to Endicott, New York to train for four months.

"Off the boat at Buffalo and then took a train on which were about 30 IBM boys and girls. I've never seen so many attractive people . . . . Then we arrived and are staying at the hotel. We all 110 people had dinner together." (Martha Smith's Diary, July 12, 1941)

The women were trained to teach men how to use the new machines and how to trouble-shoot problems. The men were trained to be salesmen. With certificate in hand and a job with IBM, Martha went to many cities to do what she had trained for and loved the range of experiences each day brought.

In 1946, Martha married a cute Navy lieutenant and left her job to begin her foray into housework and child rearing. Since she had been raised with a maid and chauffeur, Martha did not know how to keep house or cook meals. The over-full trash can stumped her; she had not grasped that all her life someone had taken care of it for her. Never having so much as boiled water before, she studied Irma S. Rombauer's 1931 *The Joy of Cooking,* and reached new heights of joy when she found Peg Bracken's *The I Hate to Cook Book* in 1960.

After the births of four kids in five years she was busy, and housework ranked low in her mind. She would have much rather read a book in her "free" time. It was a good fit for her to start a job as a library clerk to help earn money for the purse-pinched household. It also gave the family a steady stream of books to read.

For the next 30 years, Martha honed in on her kids, to encourage and support them in every way she could.

In her 60s Martha took up jogging and came in first in the 60-year-old age group of the Rialto 5K Run. As the only runner in the 60-year-old age group, she also came in dead last — just in front of the ambulance. Her grandson told her, "Grandma! They cheered more for you than for anyone else!"

Her grown children pushed her to buy a computer and didn't get why she had qualms about doing so. She took a computer-programming class at the local college, but it wasn't until she was over 80 that she bought a computer. When I asked her why she had waited so long, she said she was afraid she would love it so much that she wouldn't be able to stop using it. In the end, she changed her mind because she was a letter writer and she began to see that if she wanted to stay linked to friends and family, she needed to switch to email.

Martha died at the age of 85, five days after taking her last daily two-mile power walk.

Martha Janney Smith McGowan was a bright, gentle, optimistic woman who glowed with a zest for life. All who came in touch with her felt loved. I was blessed to have her as my mother because she loved me, backed my dreams, and stirred me to feel I could do or figure out anything. An original? Yes, she was.

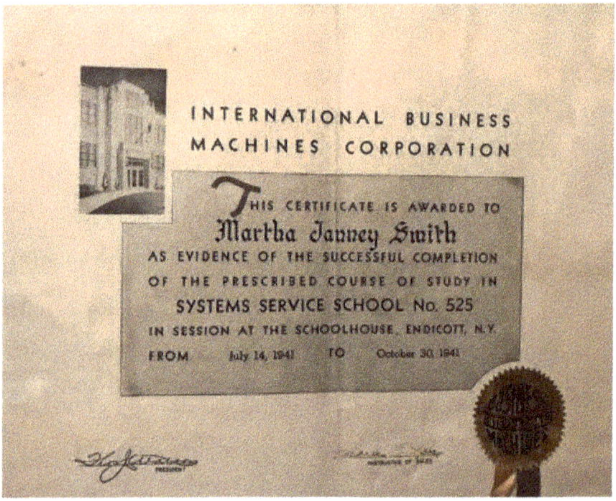

21

A Brother Like That

Shelley Pierce

He sat with us and was one of us.

Well, sort of one of us.

We were teens. And he was . . . well . . . old. He was, like, in his 40s!

We put our chairs against the wall. So did he.

We said our teachers at school were mean. He said, "I had a brother like that."

The girls said a boy was cute. He said, "I had a brother like that."

The boys said they hate work. He said, "I had a brother like that."

He made us laugh.

When we cried, he cried.

We felt safe. We were safe.

He had lifesavers in his pocket. In times of sorrow with no words. he gave me a lifesaver.

In times of joy, he gave me a lifesaver.

We opened our Bibles and held them on our laps. He opened his Bible and taught from his heart.

It began as a youth Sunday school class and grew into a family. He helped us love each other as we learned to love God. He was Jesus with skin on in our lives.

Mr. Ed listened and taught and loved and shared and gave.

He is in heaven now. What he gave to us lives on.

Forty years later, many of us in that class have kept in touch. I doubt any of us can see a lifesaver and not think of Mr. Ed. And should someone say,

"My son can't sit still"

Or
"I don't like my job"
Or
"I don't make enough money."
Can you guess what is said next?
"I had a brother like that."

22

Home of the Brave

Lisa Worthey Smith

Thanh Duong Boyer's hometown of Tan Chau, South Vietnam, did not have a fire station so every home owner had to deal with a fire the best they could. One day smoke alerted Thanh's parents of a house on fire, so they pulled their children out into to the street, then went back to gather as much as they could from their home.

Thanh, only five, but the oldest of the siblings, saw the chaos. Rather than sit and cry in fear, she took action to get her younger siblings to a safer spot. She hailed a pedicab and instructed the driver in her most adult voice: "Take them to my aunt's home. It's a couple of blocks over there. She will pay the fare when you deliver them. I promise." Thanh's parents focused on gathering items from the house until the threat passed and did not know what Thanh had done until the fire was out.

Thanh may have been small but was also powerful. She didn't just protect her family. She also saw to it that no child was bullied on "her street." After she "made a believer" out of a certain bully who picked on one of her friends, the other children called her "the enforcer."

A few years later when Vietnam fell to Communism the family lost their freedom, their jobs, and their wealth. What little gold they had hidden would have fed the eight of them for a short time, but Thanh's parents used it to send her on a boat to Australia. Their plan was for the rest of the family to join her a few months later.

The South China Sea had become a highway filled with boat people and the pirates who sought to rob them. In the rough seas, the boats often sank under the too-heavy loads. Only about half of those who tried to leave survived the trip, but if anyone could make it, Thanh could.

At 12 years old, she boarded the boat on a quest for freedom — armed with a small bag of rice, some dried fish, a change of clothes, and some bracelets to exchange for food until her family could join her Down Under. She didn't cry one tear when she left her parents and country behind. She knew she had to be brave, for her family counted on her.

Pirates attacked. When they searched her, Thanh hid her jewelry in her mouth and clenched her fists ready to "make believers" of those bullies, if need be. The pirates took all the gold they found then left those on the boat with no radio, no gas for the motor, no maps, very little food, and a huge storm on the way. Surely they will die at sea.

Death did snatch up the weak among them, and sharks circled their boat. After days adrift, they were found by a ship that towed their boat to KuKu, a small, empty Indonesian island. Thanh worked alongside the adults to find food, draw water from a stream, and make shelter.

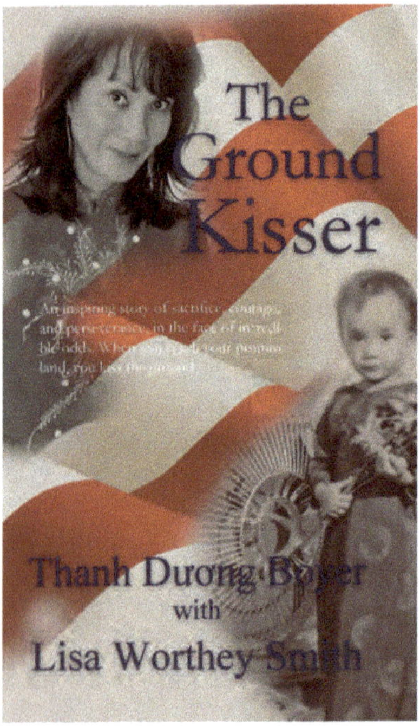

By the grace of God, she lasted a long and lean year there before coming to the USA. Instead of the few months apart that her family had planned, 15 years passed before Thanh could sponsor them to join her in the land of the free.

And as long as she lives here, it will also be the home of the brave.

23

Bill, a Friend of Jesus

Lin Daniels

His red hair hung down past his neck, a good fit for his not-so-trimmed beard. He lived in jeans and tees, dress shirts were rare for him. He was a Willie Nelson fan, and you could tell it by his garb. From one look, most would never guess that his great love was to share Jesus with folks. When not using his given name, Bill would use the intro of just being a "friend of Jesus." Never "Rev. Bill." Or "Pastor Bill."

Twice a year, Bill and his wife, Barb, would pack an old blue van with teens and trek the more than 2,600 miles from his home church in Lethbridge, Alberta to Texas. Along the way they would stop at homes of friends — and meet with small groups to pray, sing and share about what God was doing in each life. I met him at such a home visit. And not long after, he asked me to join them at Teen Camp in Canada.

I loved that when Bill talked to the teens about Jesus, he would never sugar coat his words. When I would get ready to serve at Teen Camp, I knew above all else, I would need to speak the truth. Once, after we sang, he began his "talk" with, "So Lin, have you ever been mad at God?" Mind you, I had no idea he was going to ask such a thing! And all the pairs of teen eyes were right on me! When I said "yes" in a very soft voice he piped up, "Would you like to tell us about it? " So I did. You can't fool teens; they can spot a fraud a mile away! And my heart also came back to what Bill would often quip to the teens: " Lies come in six packs!" You cannot tell just one. One lie leads to one more, and then to hide that lie, one more . . .

Bill often trekked to odd spots to tell folks about God's love. His motto in the bars was, "Talk fast and make them laugh!" Once, an angry biker group took him to a back alley, and with fists clenched were ready to pound him out. But out of the blue, the one in charge of the gang put a halt to the chaos. He said that only one other being in the whole world had told him that Jesus loved him. That was his grandmother, and all through his life she loved him the most! So the biker boss set Bill free.

Life was not easy for Bill. At 12 years old, still only a kid, he began shots to keep his sugar level at an even keel. His sight was poor, so he would trip over things. (Even his size 14 shoes could not keep him from falls!) He was quick to catch colds and felt bad for days on end. But his health never kept him from the call of God on his life. (Nor did the fact that he sang off key ever stop his love songs about Jesus!)

Near the end of his life, Bill told me his goal was to not let anger take over his heart. I found that strange, since I could not call to mind even one time when he had lost his cool! His hope was to keep a soul full of thanks. And he did!

I still hold in mind Bill's laugh, wise words, and burps. (Yep, he did have a flaw or two!) Bill was the first to ever ask me if I would like to preach, and I did so over many years at his Teen Church Camps. I think he might have had a clue that later in life I would write and preach. To this day, when I share about God, I try to be open, frank and give short talks, ala Bill. I think he would be proud!

24

Ode to Edna

Marilyn Turk

Edna loved M.L.K., J.F.K., Jesus, and me. I'm sure she loved her spouse and her sons too, but I thought I was up there with the first three.

She came to our house five days a week, rain or shine, hot or cold.

I thought she came just to see me, her fave, her girl. I did not know 'til I was a teen that she came to work. I was part of her job.

But I knew she loved me.

Tall and strong, she cleaned, washed and ironed, but did not fuss or fret. She was my rock. She was there for me when I fell, when I felt the need to talk, when I thought life was just about me. She held me when I cried, found what I had lost, shook her head when I did or said things not wise.

When I saw her, I did not see black or brown; I saw love. As she told me, "I knew yuh befo' you was born." She knew me so well, and still she loved me. No one but God knew me more.

She was like a mom but a friend too. She heard me when no one else did. She saved me from thorns, scrapes, and falls. She cared . . . and she was not paid to do that.

I thought it strange that that though she worked for my mom all those years, they were not friends. At least not to the world. But they spent days and months and years side by side. At lunch time, they watched their show; but Edna would not sit with Mom. She stood while she ate, as if she did not care. When I asked her why, she said she liked to stand and eat. I do not know if Mom had asked her to sit, but I learned as I aged that a wall was there I did not see — and did not want to see.

Time passed, I moved far from Edna, but not far from her heart. Each year when her card came on the day of my birth, I knew that she still thought of me, still loved me as I did her.

News of her death came when I was grown with babes of my own. It hit me hard. I never thought she would die. Her son called to tell me. He said she'd been sick but had not told them. That was like her, not to share her trials, so her loss was a shock to all who loved her.

Some day when I die, I'll see her. And I will not see black or brown or walls. I'll just see love.

25

One of a Kind

Susan Cheeves King

In my 27 years of teaching college English, I have worked with over 5,000 students. Most I remember fondly — if I remember them at all. Some I'm still in touch with; some I became very close to. One even lived with our family for a while.

But one stands out as a true original. Don't get me wrong. Every person is unique and thus an original. But some people sense more fully who they are and tend to reveal this more consistently, freely, and publicly than others do.

Such was Sam Koh. Now and then as our 7 A.M. class at Biola University began, Sam would bound in to greet me with, "Oh, Mrs. King! I hope you appreciate I'm here! My friend at the beach called this morning to tell me the waves are breaking at eight feet so I'm leaving right after this class." Although Sam didn't fit the blue-eyed, long-haired-blond stereotype of a California beach boy, he was an avid surfer.

For an early class assignment (a comparison-contrast essay), Sam compared two types of toilets — the typical American toilet and the more international water closet. I have to admit that no student had ever chosen that particular topic.

True originals don't make an effort to be this way. They just are who they are. Part of their charm is that they don't seem to know how much the rest of us see them as one-of-a-kind.

I came to know this when I saw its other side. One student sticks in my mind because he was so intent on being seen as an original, and that was one of the reasons that he never would be. He was full of himself, but he wasn't genuine and authentic in being that self. His name was Jason, but on the first day he decreed that I call him, "Paithen" and turned in all his work using that name. He fancied himself a Writer and in his first essay (an assignment that wasn't supposed to use sources) he actually quoted himself from something he'd written earlier. Every class day, he would wear a different hat, the most notable — and distracting — a jester's cap, complete with bells. With each act, he seemed to shout, "Look at me! I'm different." But it didn't ring true. He was just trying too hard, which doesn't fit with my view of what it means to be a true original.

Sam Koh does.

Even if Sam had dropped out of my class after the second day, I would have chosen to write this piece about him. As with every other first General Education course in English, nearly all of Sam's class was made up of freshman. Because it was held at 7 A.M. on the first day of classes in the first semester of the college year, the first day of this course had been the very first college class for most of the students in the room. They were so young, so new, so green.

To help them feel more a part of the group, on every first day of this course I would ask each student to write down and turn in an interesting fact about him/herself. Then, sometime before the next class meeting, I would compile all the answers into a list that I divided into five versions containing five different sets of facts so that I would end up with a pile of 25 half sheets.

I very well remember typing up the lists for that class since one student had written a fact unlike any I'd seen before: "This year, my father died doing what he loved. He was a pilot." I agonized about where in the list to put this fact. It just didn't seem to fit between "I once took my cat's medicine." and "I have six toes on one foot."

Then, at the start of the next class, the students — each with a half page in hand — had to go around the room trying to find out which classmate fit with each of their sheet's five facts. To do this, they couldn't just hold up the sheet in a classmate's face and ask, "Are you on here?" but instead had to engage each student in a conversation that in the end would lead to the topic of that fact.

After the time was up, the students went back to their seats and I read off each fact and then asked who had found the one who wrote that fact. When I got to the heart-wrenching one, Sam raised his hand. "It's Tom," he said, nodding toward the older student sitting to his left.

"I'm sorry," Tom said. "It wasn't the right thing to put down. It's just all I've been able to think about since we lost him. Now it's only my mom and me."

At that, Sam turned, placed his hand on Tom's arm, and said, "That's all right. We'll be your family." What newbie freshman boy *does* that?

Two years later, as I was calling the roll on the first day of that same level of English course, I saw that one of the students had the last name of "Koh." After I called his name, I began to ask him, "Do you have a brother named —"

"Sam? Yes — and I'm nothing like him!" he snapped.

A month or two later, when I ran into Sam on the campus and told him that his brother was in my class he replied, "The bum!"

It would seem that it isn't easy being the sibling of a true original.

For several years, Sam Koh has been ministering to a multi-ethnic community as the lead pastor of Hillside church in East Los Angeles where a main focus has been "to feed, clothe, inspire and love on" those who are homeless in their community. Sam is also the founder of NexGen Pastor's Fellowship, a network and organization of Asian American pastors, and is a speaker for Living Life, a daily television devotional program that airs on CGNTV. He resides in Orange, California, with his wife Shanie and their son Benji. In his free time, you can find him somewhere in the Pacific Ocean fishing or surfing some waves.

Sam Koh Today

26

Unforgettable Aunt Mary

Tony Nester

She was short and so round that she took up all the space around her and your space as well. But you didn't mind as long as you weren't one full of pride, or you hid things about yourself. At Aunt Mary's table, food was love. Food led to smiles, sighs, and tales of how you did this or that brave or bad thing, while those at the table with you gave a tease or a grunt that was code for "You did good!" I liked Aunt Mary's table more than the one at my house where we didn't talk much and laughed even less.

When I was 12 years old my mother died, and Aunt Mary said I could live with her. My Dad was glad to let me go, but my older sister, Rose, said "No, Tony comes with me." In the fight over me that came next, Aunt Mary won. My Uncle Fritz said "okay" and cousin Frank and cousin Gary gave up some room for me. At first, I slept with Gary. One night after we were asleep, Aunt Mary came into our bedroom with two big banana splits and said she thought we might like ice cream. It was the only time in my life I've had ice cream in bed — and with cherries and whipped cream, too!

It didn't work out very long for me to sleep with Gary. Aunt Mary made a bed for me on a couch in what used to be a porch. My aunt's family was kind to me, but still I knew it wasn't my family. When Frank left home, Fritz and Mary and Gary would sit in the front seat of their Buick while I sat in the back. I would stare at the back of their heads and feel far away.

Aunt Mary found lots of ways to save money. She sprayed her old wood furniture with Crackle to make it look new. She liked electric ranges since the burners gave "free" heat when you turned them off. When she cleaned other people's houses for money, she took baths in their bathtubs to save on her water bill at home. With no shame, we children took food home from the dump behind the grocery store. No food went to waste; Aunt Mary turned all scraps into snacks, treats, or sandwiches. Her purse could always produce a small meal on the go.

Clothes just didn't count for much. Poor Frank didn't get a Boy Scout uniform to match his Scout-friends because the family had no money for it. He says he decided then and there never to be poor . . . and he never has been. He always wears nice clothes. Back then I didn't know we were poor. Aunt Mary never used that word.

Once I found a photograph of Aunt Mary when she was young, had an hour-glass shape, and a look that would catch a man's eye. *When did she turn round and fat?* I don't know. Nor do I know how my Uncle Fritz felt about her. She had a three-piece pink whole-body vibration machine down the stairs that some said could make your fat go away if you lay on it and let it shake you all over. I gave it a try. It didn't work for me, nor did it work for Aunt Mary. But she kept it.

Every week or two, Fritz's brother, Orlando, brought him a paper sack full of books which my uncle put away. I never once saw my uncle with a book in his hands, but one day I found the books in a bathroom cupboard and I read one. Girls were taking off their clothes one piece at a time in a card game with men, and then standing naked in a line by a wall. I knew my Uncle Fritz was good at cards. Aunt Mary didn't seem to mind when Orlando brought the paper sacks, although later I found out that Mary and Fritz had lived apart for a time.

Aunt Mary was an ex-Catholic-born-again Christian and took my mother, Sarah, to the same revival service that she went to. So Mary, Sarah, and their children no longer talked "Catholic" with our Catholic-Italian clan. Aunt Mary fed me the Bible along with her pasta, gnocchi, and anchovy pizza. My own path into the ministry goes back to her ready joy over "The Word." Who better to teach me to "*taste and see that the Lord is good*" (Psalm 34:8 NIV)?

After Uncle Fritz died, a cancer began to grow in Aunt Mary's stomach. Surgeons cut it out more than once, but it always grew back. Only one guess what my Aunt thought to do: cure herself with food, of course! She found a clinic in Mexico that filled her with "anti-cancer" food that made her feel good. They also had sweet music and lots of good thoughts. But food didn't cure her cancer, and the doctors said no to do any more surgeries.

Aunt Mary did not fear to die since she knew she would see Jesus — and my mother, Sarah. She would feast at the Table of the Lord. Frank and Gary asked me to come and preach her funeral. It wasn't hard to do because it was my Aunt Mary who gave me love and food and an early taste of faith.

I know so much more than Aunt Mary ever did. I've gone to good schools, read lots of books, made friends with some very smart people, found love, and have a family of my own. My mind can grasp some very big thoughts and turn them over this way and that. I've not been poor in any way. But still today I wish I could sit at Aunt Mary's table and will always be glad that I once did.

27

The Soloist

Reba Rhyne

Jimmy wasn't trained as a singer, but he did have a booming voice which could carry a tune, and he loved to sing. He placed no limits on where or when he might burst into song. Since he was a Christian, one would truly think of church, maybe a choir or group. I can imagine him singing in the car or in the bath, both usual places to lift your voice in song — but the grocery store?

In the late 1950s, the store was large, locally-owned, and well-known — with each part given to the varied and usual sections we see in any store today. Back then, people would tend to shop on the same day, week after week. They saw it as a chance to catch up with friends or even family — those you didn't see often. So some major hitch or just being ill would keep them from it.

Jimmy would show up on his day as well. He and his wife, Bess, were not thin people. He was balding, tall, and out-going. His shoes were buffed until they shone. She wore her dress below her knees, with purse on her arm, and a smile on her face.

On coming in the double-front doors of the mart and before starting his trek though the store aisles, Jimmy always greeted the ladies on the check-out stands. Bess might or might not be with him. If she wasn't with him his hand clasped a list of needed items, clearly seen as he pulled out a metal cart and started down the produce aisle. That's when it would start — the song, I mean . . .

"There's a call comes ringing o'er the restless wave,
Send the light! Send the light!

There are souls to rescue, there are souls to save,
Send the light! Send the light!"

While singing, Jimmy would pick out the bananas Bess had written on the list — slightly green and no black spots. He didn't buy tomatoes or green onions since he grew them in his garden at home, but he did look at them, making sure his home-grown ones were of higher value, while singing the chorus . . .

"Send the light! The blessed gospel light.
Let it shine, from shore to shore.
Send the light, the blessed gospel light.
Let it shine from shore to shore."

By now, he would be at the meat market, standing before the beef mounded in trays. He would pause at the meat counter long enough to order six pounds of meat for making hamburgers in three two-pound packs from the man on the other side. *Let's see — three pounds for a dollar — so two dollars*; he would check it off the list. Then it was on to the pork case for 16 pork chops in two packs. He made it clear to the clerk that Bess liked the big ones with lots of fat; they made good milk gravy. That would be the extent of his meat buys. Oh, except for four pounds of sausage. (It wasn't on the list, but it was on sale. His wife would give him an extra hug for this.)

At this point, the music would often cease and one and all in the store knew Jimmy had found a friend to talk to. Some tics later, chat ended, he neared the pre-packed meats. Second verse . . .

"We have heard the Macedonian call today,
Send the light! Send the light!
And a golden offering at the cross we lay.
Send the light! Send the light.

Into the buggy went two packs of hot dogs, two pounds of bacon, and fat-back for cooking the green beans he'd pick from his garden.

Send the light! The blessed gospel light.
Let it shine, from shore to shore.
Send the light! The blessed gospel light.
Let it shine from shore to shore."

The song's third verse went with him down the aisles on his way to find the canned goods, cake mixes, and frosting on Bess's list.

"Let us pray that grace may everywhere abound.
Send the light! Send the light!
And a Christ-like spirit everywhere be found.
Send the light! Send the light!"

By the time he got to the dairy cases where he put two gallons of milk, one gallon of buttermilk, three dozen eggs, two pounds of butter, and sliced cheese into his now-full cart, he would mouth," Oh, don't let me forget rolls, sliced bread and buns for the meat" and start on the last verse.

"Let me not grow weary in the work of love.
Send the light! Send the light!
Let us gather jewels for a crown above.
Send the light! Send the light!"

On the way to the check-out lane, he would end with the chorus . . .

"Send the light! The blessed gospel light.
Let it shine, from shore to shore.
Send the light! The blessed gospel light.
Let it shine forevermore."

For as long as I worked at that store, Jimmy came every Friday after work. The song might not have been the same each time, but you could be sure you would be crooned to as soon as his hands grabbed a cart. And, if you heeded closely, you would hear the Gospel message, the Light of the world, proclaimed every time he was in the store. True, it's not the usual place to hear it uttered, above all not by song. But that was Jimmy's way.

28

Thank You, Ms. Reed

Michelle Ruschman

I was in my teens the first time I sat in Ms. Phyllis Reed's English class. It was 1985 at Wagner High School on Clark Air Base in the Philippines. By the time she put her eyes on me I had come to know that some grown men had it in them to hurt small kids. I also knew what it was like to think of food as a friend, and I used the fat on my body as a wall to keep away the boys who might hurt me. I was in full "shields-up" mode with a smile that was open more than a crack, but back then I never let it rest on my face. As a kid with a family in the U.S. Air Force, I learned how to leave friends and to keep my heart hard. This young bee knew not to stay on one petal for very long.

When I was little, I liked to write. At the age of six, I wrote a story that Mrs. Chase liked so much she read it to the class. It felt good to hear my words read by an adult who liked to smile at me while she read them. By the time Ms. Reed met me though, that day had been long lost in the faded blur of hurts gone by. It took Ms. Reed to show me that words could make me want to smile again — a more open smile this time — and see the worth in what I had to say. All those years, the words had lined up in my pen ready for Ms. Reed to give me a way to let them know the joy of being on paper again. They poured out of me in poetry, speech, and essay. Then Ms. Reed would smile as I, or she, would read each one aloud.

Ms. Reed was a tall woman who took up *space* — and not only with the width of her thick body. She filled a room with her wide-open grin and her verve. Her eyes would lock onto yours so you knew she *saw* you. Not one of us failed to *feel* her as soon as we would enter our room. Her voice boomed, and in the clipped way she talked, every "t" sound popped at the end of her words. Her skin was a rich umber made dark by the hot Philippine sun. Since our school was so small, I had Ms. Reed every year for the three years we were at Clark. Her class was the best part of my day and among my best times ever while we lived there.

One day, I wore a black cowl-neck top to school, and Ms. Reed told me — this flat-faced fat Filipino teen — that I looked like a model. She made me feel that it was true. Through the lens of her eyes, for the first time, I saw a glow in me. She made me feel new and fresh — not broken down and small.

Ms. Reed pulled me out of my own head and helped me find my voice. In her class I began to love being in front of others, to give a speech and even to teach. In the front of her room the fear in me began to shrink. The little girl in me began to grow up.

I wish I could find Ms. Reed today and hug her neck. I hear she's a woman of the cloth these days; that doesn't shock me at all. She talks life into all people now, not just kids, and I have no doubt that they hang on her every word as she speaks with the love of Jesus — the way she did when I was a teen. If I can't tell her face to face, I'll tell her here: "Thank you, Ms. Reed, for what you did to help me heal even on the days when all you did was to be present to teach me."

29

Minnesota "Bear Man"

Terry Magness

In the summer of 1991, when our friends Chuck and Marsha asked us to join them at his boss's place on Lake Vermillion in Minnesota, we were pumped. We caught so many fish the first three days, we were in need of a break. So our friends took us for a little drive. Chuck turned off a main road near Orr, onto a dirt-and-grass lane flanked by woods. A metal farm gate stood wide open as if to wave us in.

With a you-don't-know-what-I-know grin that stretched from ear to ear, Chuck crowed, "We're about there."

Marsha added, "You're not going to *believe* this!"

Our car made its way down the strange dirt lane, until all at once the trees gave way to two cleared acres in the midst of the woods. Off to one side sat an old mobile home and a car that looked as if it had seen its best days. Close by stood a lone form.

The aged man moved to the wreck of a car and stood by its door. He looked quite usual in his shirt tucked into worn jeans held by red suspenders. His ball cap — "Duffy" stitched on its front — hid most of his white hair. But we were soon to find out that not one thing about this man or this place was usual.

As our eyes scanned the area, we spied at least 20 black bears, 12 of them cubs, as they roamed the grounds. Two of the large bears who had seen the man walk to the car trailed him there. One of the bears, which must have weighed at least 700 pounds, reared up on the caved-in trunk of the car. It gave under his weight. The other bear, just as large if not more, climbed onto the hood, or what was left of it, and put his front paws on its roof. The man's eyes were huge, round and bugged, as he stared toward my camera through the dark rimmed, thick-glass specs perched on his nose.

No one else is here, I thought. *He needs our help.* Yet I dared not move.

Minnesota logger Vince Shute, born in 1913, was in fact quite at home with his four-pawed neighbors and they with him. Vince never forgot that these were wild bears, but they all got along well from shared respect.

This had not been the case in Vince's logging camp back in the late 30s. He and his men dealt daily with bears who pushed, clawed, and smashed their way into the camp's cook shed to get at the food. The men shot many bears, and still they came.

After years of failed tries to stop the raids, Vince's thoughts changed. "Bears are not mean — just hungry," he was heard to say.* So the young logger set out to find a way to live in peace with his hungry neighbors. The thought came to him, *What if I could lure the bears away with food?* We know now to never, ever, feed bears. But in those days, Vince didn't know this. He set food out in front of the cook shack, and the bears took it but didn't break in. His plan worked! That was the start of 50 years of feeding bears. What began as a way to put an end to bear raids turned into a "labor of love."*

Vince spent most of his money on food for the bears until local shops and cafes began to give what they could. It was all stored in his car.

The bears poised on top of his car that day were waiting for their daily snack of corn, left-over donuts, and chocolate milk which he put out for them in gallon cartons and often fed 50 or more bears.

Vince called all the bears his friends; yet only a few were close to the logger. He gave them all names. One of his choice friends was Duffy, an 800-pound black bear, that Vince said was the only bear he could touch. Duffy was the bear on top of the car that first day. We met him — *after* snack time.

Vince shared this story with us, about another friend named Brownie: "The bear came to me badly hurt. I took care of his wounds and nursed him back to health. Winter came on before he was well, so he hibernated under my place [his trailer] 'til spring."

In Orr the next day, I picked up a local postcard, with a photo taken by the Associated Press. It showed Vince with a slice of cinnamon bread clenched in his teeth and Duffy, ready to take a bite of it. By the mid 80s, Vince was known to the locals as "the Bear Man."*

In the fall of 1993 (about the time of our second visit), as his health began to fail, 80-year-old Vince and three friends — who also cared what would befall "his" bears after he was gone — began a work to form what would, in January 1995, come to be The American Bear Association. It is a nonprofit organization that runs The Vince Shute Wildlife Sanctuary where more than 20,000 people now come every summer to see the bears.*

In his last years, Vince lived in a care home in Orr but visited his bears when he could. We heard that Duffy was killed during the 1998 bear season. Vincent Shute, a Minnesota bear man, died on July 4, 2000 at the age of 86, happy that his bears were being well cared for.

*The American Bear Association, https://www.americanbear.org/the-sanctuary/history/

30

No Words

Alice H. Murray

I didn't know her name, and she didn't know mine. I didn't know how old she was or where she was born. I didn't know who her mom and dad were; I knew only that they weren't able to care for her. She lived in Guatemala in a home for kids with no kin to care for them.

We had a brief time face to face one July eight years ago, and ever since then, I haven't been able to get her out of my mind. I don't think that I ever will or could. How is it that a young child with whom I spent less than half an hour could leave such a vivid image and tug at my heart so?

I had come to Guatemala from Florida with a group of those of my faith. All of us knew Jesus and meant to show His love to kids in Central America. I came to help, but I was not sure just how I was going to do that. I could not build, sew, or even speak Spanish. But I was there and did what tasks I was asked to do. I cut fruit for meals, swept, and cleared the shelves of old meds which could not be used.

Then one day after lunch I was given a new task. I had to carry a box down the hill to the place where the kids from the home were in class. The box had items in it for them to wear. I was to leave the box and then go back to the room where I had been at work. It was a nice day, and I was happy to be out in the sun. The area by the home was green and full of flora. At the foot of the hill I found a room where I put the box down and then left to head back up the hill.

Some kids had come out of class and were also set to climb the hill. I heard them laugh and speak in Spanish, but I had no idea what they said. And then I saw her — a small, thin girl of maybe six or seven with dark hair and big eyes. She was alone. I gave her a smile, and she gave me one. As timid as a mouse, she came close to me. Our eyes met. I knew no Spanish, and she knew no English. But we both knew how to smile. We could talk with our eyes and with smiles. Shyly she put out her hand and took mine. Again we each gave the other a smile.

The two of us went up the hill side by side. She was aware I had come a long way to help her and the other kids at the home. We did not have to talk for her to know that. In her eyes I could see that she was happy that I was there. We could not say in words what we felt, but it was clear that we cared for each other. Even if I had known Spanish, I am not sure that I could have said all that was in my heart. What a dear child! She had no mom or dad, but she knew what love was. She knew that my being there was an act of love.

At last we came to the top of the hill. When she got to the door where she had to leave me, she gave me a huge smile and took her time to let go of my hand. Then she went in. I did not see her after that. Her life went on, and so did mine.

How I still ache for that child! She had so much love to give, and she seemed to long for a mother's touch. Where is she now? Is she okay? I will never know. I won't feel her touch on my hand again, but I will ever feel her touch on my heart. I pray that God will watch over her. He is love and that is Who and what she needs most of all.

31

Choosing Joy

Marilyn Switzer

She can talk to a post, and if the post could speak it would swear that it had just met its new best friend. If you meet her, soon you will know tales of her life, for she loves to share them. Mary Williams has known life on this earth near 95 years, and she has met each dawn with the words, "This day I choose joy."

Those who meet her are shocked to learn her age. She does not look it. She has great hair. When folks ask, "Are those your own teeth?" she says, "Yes, each one." She has blue eyes that can flash and give you the stink eye if she feels you need it. She has a style that she did not get from her mom; nor did she pass it down to her own girls. She loves good style in the clothes she wears, in the home she shares, in the gifts she gives, in the food she cooks, in the life she lives. Her feet hurt all the time, but even so, she must have shoes with style.

Friends seek her out. Mary is great fun. She loves the news. She can't see how those of us who don't watch the news can know whom to vote for. But we don't have to watch the news; we just go to her to find out. She loves sweets and has no hard and fast rule about them, so she may share or she may not. Most days she has pain in her neck, her back, her leg, and of course her feet. She plays down the pain and goes on her blithe way.

Even on days of bad pain, she still grits her teeth and says, "This day I choose joy."

She's had lots of jobs; three she liked most. A man who owned a quite posh store asked her to wear the clothes they sold so that those who shopped there would want to spend more. When the man asked her to work more time, she quit, for she had babes at home and yearned to be with them. When TV came on the scene, she was hired to do live ads. Once on live TV as she tried to cut a steak, it was so tough that it flew off the plate down to the floor. She thought for sure she would be fired, but she wasn't. In fact, her boss got quite a charge from it, for he knew that no one who had seen that ad would soon get his brand of steaks out of their minds.

When the Nashville boom came, she hired some girls to give tours, for her and her name was soon known to all who did the same sort of work. Mary had the best guides in town, and she was glad to tell you

so. She loved those tours. It is a bit of a hoot that she led folks around town, for she was not well versed in how to find the right paths. If she got a bus full of guests lost, her charm and smooth words would soon have those folks thrilled at the new route. She at last quit work when some would have called her old. But she says that she just now might be close to old. She would love to wear those clothes, do those ads, lead those tours; but her age tells her she can't. Yet even as she so longs for work, she still says, "This day I choose joy."

She has a mule's will and often can be heard to say that she will "risk it." She does not ask for help, as she wants to "do it" on her own. "If you quit," she says, "it's hard to start back," so she does not quit. She drives to the store, buys her goods, brings them home, then takes them from the trunk of her car to her house — one piece at a time. As she toils up those steps on the last trip she says, "This day I choose joy."

Mary has known great bliss and has been stunned by great grief. When asked if she has kids, she says, "Yes, five," though she has laid to rest two sons. One died of ill health, one at his own hand. The grief that came with this last loss could have done her in. For a time, she would roam her street in the dead of night. As she wept and cried to God, she tried to make sense of the pain she felt. She stored the ache in her heart and did not cast it on her friends. At the end of each walk, she would go to bed, and at the break of dawn, she would wake and say with that iron will of a mule, "This day I choose joy."

I call Mary Williams Mom. She has taught me much. Most of all, I hope that I, too, can learn to greet each day with joy.

32

Why Aren't We Dancing?

Jill Allen Maisch

Jim. I met him at a homeless shelter where he was a client and I a volunteer. I had gone to serve a hot meal, and while I was there Jim served me the story of his life. He had lived through years of grief and pain — some due to bad luck, but most due to bad choices.

Jim showed up at our church one Sunday. He sat way in the back, and I went to sit with him. As we sang the hymn, "Lord of the Dance," he looked at me and asked, "Why aren't we dancing?" *Good point*, I thought. So, we stood up, linked arms, and did a few twirls. Some people stared, but I didn't care. It felt like the right thing to do, and I could sense that God was smiling.

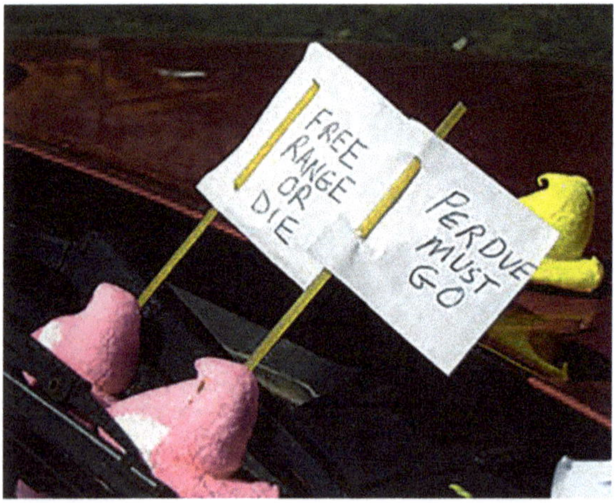

Jim loved to play pranks. One Easter I came out of church to find a line of ten marshmallow Peeps on the hood of my car. Some held small signs that read "I am not a dumb chick" or "Free range or die," or "Purdue must go." I knew it had to be Jim, and I was right. I spied him not too far away in his old, beat up car with a huge smile on his face.

Later that year Jim found out he had skin cancer. He had let it go too long, and the doctors had given him just one or two months to live. In spite of the pain, he still played pranks on folks and still came to church. That last Sunday he was quite frail. He sat hunched over in his wheelchair with me next to him on the pew. I was thrilled that the hymn that day was "Lord of the Dance." As we began to sing, he turned to me and with a smirk asked, "Why aren't we dancing?" Even though he was so weak, we still hooked arms and I gently turned his wheelchair in a circle.

When we got close to Easter this year, the sight of Peeps in all the stores brought Jim to my mind. And at church the next Sunday we sang "Lord of the Dance." As we began to sing, I turned to a friend near me and asked, "Why aren't we dancing?" So, we linked arms and did a spin. Some people stared, but I didn't care. This time I was sure that God and Jim were both smiling.

33

Hope in a Red Hat

Leah Hinton

"Put your nose down. Do good work." This is what I was taught. "No room for big dreams. The world is hard as it is. Don't make it worse with fancy ideas."

But I did dream. Those dreams took the back seat to all of my other roles, at work, as wife, as mom. But the dreams were still a part of me, even if they stirred only at the outer edge of my mind. That is, until the day they didn't. Until the day they rose to the top of my thoughts.

My soul said write. I did. The gates were wide open. Words flowed, but they were born of what? I didn't know. Who did what? I couldn't keep track. Text, plot, arc. I had to learn, so I took a class. Yet when I saw those with great gifts, I felt more dim than the one dead bulb above the table.

But hope crept into my mind with one glance from a woman with a big smile and kind eyes. She wore a red cowgirl hat, red boots, and red shirt with a west-Texas flair. This woman in red would change my life. Her name is Arianne Thompson.

In the days of dial-up internet, her mother had her choose a screen name which would not alert would-be bad-guys as to who she was. "Texas-Two-Step" was taken, so she chose Tex2S. The name fit well and in that early teen time, a life-long identity was born. Arianne would then and always be Tex.

Her happy red hat and the Texas lilt in her voice were not the only things that drew me to her. She had a ton of love and bold drive in her face. With one gaze at her smile — one that lit up her eyes — all my doubts about being in that room were gone.

She fought my mystic beasts of doubt and ran through the tinny, lost voice in my head with a sword of hope and joy. Dreams were not a far-off thing. They were gifts worth the chase. She laid bare and built the keystone of my art. And she is crazy smart, to boot.

Her mantra is easy. "Chase dreams. Never squash what should be built up. Honor the brave who would try." And there is "No nope."

This woman's mind is deep. It winds its genius through every task she takes on. Above all, she uses her brain for good.

She is the author of an epic wild-west fantasy trilogy. When she wrote this epic, she set up no daily word-count goals that were the ideal of her peers. But who can fault the lack of speed when the words she weaves shine in the ways they are strung tight, where they are meant for us to savor and roll about on the tongue? Her genius shows in her work, and though she is a meek woman, it speaks to her bold soul.

What fires Tex's life's work is to share her trip into the world of books as a map for us all. She enters our lives as the writer's trail-guide. Tex has a heart for those who seek their dreams and she swears it takes real guts to go out of the bounds of what is easy. She says no one should ever feel as if she can't be seen or as if he is not heard. Tex shares her gifts and joy with all she meets. And her goal is that all she meets should be better for knowing her. She looks up to Mr. Rodgers from *Mr. Rodgers' Neighborhood.* He didn't preach his values from the TV screen; he lived them. She strives to do that in every part of her life. She gives —and never with an ounce of regret. She lives a good life so that others may also.

Tex says that no author starts out good but must work to learn her craft. If an author is brave at the start, then one day that author will be glad he took the chance to do what wasn't easy.

Tex says her parents never taught her shame and that is the key to so many of her wins in life. She was free to try all the whims of her heart until she found her place — and with no regret.

Tex says that if we tell kids that they can reach their dreams, then they just might do it! For all artists in her path, she is their proud Mama — hope in a red hat.

34

No Time Left

David Buster

A world at war is a world at its worst — and such a waste. Lives lost. Homes on fire. Dreams put down and never picked up again. Any good that comes out of the chaos is a gift, a rare chance — but one which many would trade for peace if they could.

During the Great War, Dad made the most of his chance to enter med school at 16. He met and dated mom, played sports, and worked hard. While in class he saw death; he never had to see it the ways those who had to fight in the war did. After World War II ended, his exams went on for four more years. One post-grad year later, he was ready — to join the Navy and serve with the Marines in Korea.

He never talked much about the war, but I saw the slides he took with the Nikon he bought in Japan. I can still see the photo with the red hair on his upper lip. Snow-topped latrine seats in a line over a trench. And blood — from wounds of every kind. Many an image from a young man who never told his son why he got the medal he wore.

The years that doctors train after med school are not called school, but that's what they are. After Korea, Dad trained as a surgeon and earned 30 bucks a month to work 100 hours a week as he learned to take out tumors and sick body parts that could not be saved.

In later years I would often see his photo in the local paper. He served two terms as chief of staff at our hospital. He went on rounds to teach others and judged claims on the state board. He would put his son on speed dial to join him for 3 A.M. OR cases. He knew I couldn't say no. Music would play as tubes were pushed, and lines would drip meds and blood. Now and then, we would hear a joke to calm the nerves amid time to cut, time to cure. Clamps and sharps passed back and forth. "How are your kids?" one would ask. The clock would let us know why our backs were so stiff.

Hide and go seek is a kids' game played by adults in war and peace. In peace the hero dons a mask to hide in the OR. In war, masks are stripped off and the hero is marked with a medal that hides in a box when peace breaks out.

Dad was never far from the front lines in Korea and camped with the Marines he served. I knew that much but didn't hear the story about the medal until I gave the talk at church when he died. My nephew found and read the note Dad never showed me. A busy day for me was to treat 30 folks. Dad's medal marked a day in which he set up near the front lines, then gave aid to and led back to base over 200 Marines who were too hurt to fight. Going back again, he dodged heavy shell fire to get one last Marine too banged up to walk out on his own.

Dad could call me at 3 A.M. to join him for a time to cut and a time to cure. But he never set aside a time to talk about his medal. I had to hear about it after there was no time left.

35

Bigger than the Dark

Nicey T. Eller

When the cold, clear drops of Holmes Creek streamed off my nine-year-old head onto Brother Peacock's hands and chest, I took a deep breath, wiped my face dry with the soft cloth he gave me, and grinned at my soaked friends who were lined up on the bank.

No one wore a white gown that day at the Miller's Ferry boat ramp. But we did rise from death unto life, washed in the blood and cooled off by the creek — in jeans cut off at mid-thigh and tops that clung to us the way the old folks clung to hand fans in August.

Gertrude Weaver, a giant of the faith whom we thought might have taught Shadrach, Meshach, and Abednego, stood in the shade with the crowd of saints from Live Oak Baptist Church. She knew that creek; she knew us, and we all knew that no one else was like her.

In 1939, when Mrs. Weaver turned 19, the law said she could teach, and so she did. While her pupils were out of school, she drove 245 miles away to Gainesville to take every class she lacked in being able to put "Bachelor of Science" after her name. It took ten years.

In the 1950's no bridge spanned Holmes Creek. So to get to work, Mrs. Weaver had to put her car on the ferry with Mr. Ed Skipper and float from the west side of the creek to the east side. One day Mr. Ed was not well and told Mrs. Weaver he would leave the ferry tied up for her so she could put her car on it and get home after work.

By the time she and her four-year-old daughter, Cheryl, got to the creek bank to board the ferry, the sun had bowed out in favor of the moon. And the ferry was not there.

Mrs. Weaver knew the only way to get home was to cross the creek.

She placed a light in Cheryl's hand and strict words in her ears. She was to hold that light so her mama could see as she swam the creek. She was to stay right where Mrs. Weaver left her, light in hand, to show the way.

Cheryl watched her mama kick off her shoes, wade into the water, and push off — head high. The pull of the creek didn't make her change course. Stroke after stroke, she glanced back to be sure the light was right where it should be. When she reached the boat ramp, she undid the ferry, put it on course, and kept her eyes on the light. Thoughts of what might have been in the creek and what the dark might have held did not deter her.

Over the next 43 years, as she saw kids and then their kids from one grade to the next, Mrs. Weaver was a force of love and grit. She stood alone when she had to, even when it cost her. It took guts to join the Florida teacher's strike in 1968, when the fight wasn't over money for pay but for basic needs for kids all over the state. She knew these kids were worth the fight.

She went toe to toe with those who didn't honor "Posted" signs on her land. At times that got ugly. When she dug her heels in, she brought down fire. Mrs. Weaver sang in the choir, kept the church books, and prayed for souls at home and far away. She didn't mind asking, "Why?" even when no one else would.

When my brother ran for superintendent of schools, he wanted her in his camp. She was wise as well as savvy about local races. Yet, he said that her breath came to a halt when he told her he would run as a Republican. Stone cold quiet reigned for quite a time. Then she told him she had sworn to her grandmother on her death bed that she would never vote for a Republican. God might erase their sins, but what they had done to the South after the War Between the States was seared on her grandmother's heart. Mrs. Weaver did not need books to tell what it had been like. Her grandmother knew first hand. Mrs. Weaver kept her word — except in 2012.

That's when my brother rode in a parade with Mrs. Weaver in the seat next to him and knew if he never did any other thing right, he had that day. As they wound their way on the route; kids, moms, dads, and grandparents called out to her. She waved and loved them right back. She, not my brother, was the story.

She voted for him, and when he took his oath of office, she held the Bible for him.

When there is no light, the dark feeds fear that can slow steps, crush nerves, and turn one's heart into an anvil. You can't live 97 years and not have dark times. When Mrs. Weaver gave Cheryl that light and a job to focus on, she knew that the light she gave her daughter wasn't going to help her swim to the ferry on the other side of Holmes Creek. She gave Cheryl that light and a job to be sure Cheryl would stay where she'd left her.

When Mrs. Weaver left us, we knew how to drive away the dark with the same light she sang about when she taught us "This Little Light of Mine." We knew how to swim against the stream even when it was hard, and we knew how to let go with grace.

36

Cliffhanger

Nancy Brashear

A small child points up.
"Look up there! Look! Look!"

Three barefoot boys
(three black wetsuits, one white towel),
shadows scale skyward
up a marble-cake cliff.
The crowd gasps.
Cirque du Soleil stars
with no harnesses or safety nets,
they cling
to nothing.

Dirt and stones
spill a hundred feet down
nudged by toes seeking a niche
in the high crag.

"God help them," someone prays,
and witnesses cover their eyes and camera lenses.

Did the boys shut their eyes, too?
Did they, at this same time,
feel the enormity of their actions?

The helicopter views its prey,
scatters grit and small rocks,
and whips the air
with angry chopper blades.
A firefighter drops
from the belly of the hovering craft
like a spider on its thread of silk.

One boy up, two cry.
Two boys up, one prays.
Three boys up, none left.
Abandoned blue and orange boogie boards
they'd pushed above
stuck to the cliff like post-it notes.

The crowd breathes out
a long sigh of relief.
"That'll be one nice $10,000 Father's Day bill!"
a man jokes.

The dark puddle at the base of the cliff
pools into a ropy shape and slinks down
into a tide pool.
Death is not welcome here
today.

37

From the Shadows

Ken Proctor

My son Tim is easy to lose in a crowd. Not his fault, really — he's just built that way, short of stature. "Vertically challenged" the PC crowd would say. He takes after his mother's father, so has been placed in the front row of every class photo from kindergarten, to 12th grade, and the U.S. Navy's corpsman school on Lake Michigan.

Actually, "designed that way" might be a finer way to phrase it. God blessed Tim with a big heart, but a wealth of short, at both ends, though that's not his only challenge. For reasons known only to God, Tim doesn't see the world as most of his peers do. His brain just isn't wired that way. His mechanical-reasoning skills and spatial-relationship scores are off the charts, as they say — but in the wrong direction. Even mundane tasks, like tying shoes or adding a leaf to a table, can be a tall order. Swap out a door knob? No way.

I used to joke that Tim "couldn't organize a two-horse parade" — that is until, years later, we came to see that he really couldn't. But it's not for lack of trying, mind you. He just couldn't see it; he couldn't sort through the jumble of mixed info the world fed him each moment of the day. For him, making sense of sights, sounds, and verbal instructions is like being showered by Lucky Charms and Alpha-Bits cereals and having to grasp meaning from the avalanche of mixed letters and colored shapes. Green clovers, pink hearts, blue moons.

Still, God is good, and He blessed Tim in other ways — his out-of-this-world memory, for one. His remarkable recall would allow him to get through school and earn his diploma. But using what he has learned is still hit or miss. Add to this, the fact that his ability to organize what comes out of his brain is, oddly, unimpaired, and his poetry is both perceptive and poignant.

Tim's chief gift, though, is music. Our home has never been without a piano, and Tim showed an early interest and aptitude for playing it. By age four he could play with both hands. By seven he played scores from TV shows by ear and by eight he composed original pieces. With one part of his brain — the sci-fi part — he could watch *Star Trek* reruns while the other part would dash off music on the piano keys.

About then, we signed him up for lessons so he could learn to read music and, maybe, write the scores he created. After four years of lessons with Mrs. Chandler, he could sight read Beethoven and Mozart, but, sadly, couldn't give directions to Mrs. Chandler's house from two blocks away. Yet, even 15 years later Tim's classmates remember him. Two events his senior year thrust him into the lime light and sealed him in their memories. And it all began with a girl, a crush, and a song.

Each year, students at Tim's high school may enter a talent show with a $50 top prize. Tim signed up. When his turn came, he walked on stage, sat at the piano, and told them the title of his original composition. *Alana's Dream*. The haunting, achingly sweet melody that followed stunned those there. These six minutes of passion and power were so unexpected from the boy they thought they knew. He won the prize but, alas, not Alana's heart.

That spring, as graduation plans fell into place, the principal, Mr. Delamarter, asked Tim for a favor. As part of the annual graduation ceremony, a 20-minute slide show would showcase events in the grads' final year. "Would you mind playing the piano, backstage, during the slide show? It can be whatever you want to play." Tim said he would.

The evening arrived, the commencement commenced and, at the right time, Tim slipped backstage, set up his sheet music, and waited. The auditorium lights dropped; the crowd of kids and parents hushed; the first slide flicked on the screen, and Tim played. For a solid 20 minutes, Tim played. As images of school plays, school sports, and class clowns faded from one to the next, Tim played — with no faults, no missed notes, not even a break as one unique melody flowed seamlessly into the next — *unique* because they were all original pieces, *seamless* because he knew them all by heart.

As the slides ended, Mr. Delamarter took the stage and told us that as the room's lights dropped for the show, all the lights backstage had been cut, too. "Tim Proctor," he said, "just played the entire 20 minutes, ad lib, in total darkness. Come on out here, Tim."

To a standing ovation from teachers, staff, parents, and peers, Tim parted the stage drapes and stepped out from the shadows.

38
Jesus' Texas Girl

Amy Lynn Taylor

You can pick out her sing-song Texas twang in any crowd, and her news is just as clear. "Jesus loves you," Bonnie says. It's how she'll greet you — her way to say "Hi."

Since Bonnie has a style all her own, some will not look past the quirks they don't grasp to hear her words. She wears hats with wide brims perched on dark brown hair teased and piled high like a bee's hive. Under gobs of loose clothes, her curves are lost. So are her eyes — behind dark, round shades. All she wears is black, white, or cream, but I think I caught a splash of red once. You won't know it by just looks, but those worn black boots — her only pair of shoes? — cover bare feet; she has no need for socks.

"Jesus loves you," Bonnie says. It's her love note to the world.

Next to where Bonnie eats, you might find an open seat. Don't sit there; it's saved for her best Friend. If she puts a gift in your hands, it could vary from an Oral Roberts prayer cloth to items from the Avon line, but the tag will never fail to read, "From Jesus." Bonnie's a mom to five kids. They each bear the name of a city in Texas. And it's not just her kids; her pets do, too. Over the years, she's owned all kinds of dogs and birds, but the best were a pair of doves named Mr. and Mrs. Texas.

Bonnie makes her home at 8,000 feet above sea level, among dark green pine trees and rutty chalk cliffs. The snow months keep her from going past her front yard, so she cares for her pets both wild and tame. But as soon as the earth thaws and she can drive into town, you'll find her where most don't dare go.

"Jesus loves you," Bonnie says. To those with tears on their cheeks and hurt in their hearts, she's Christ in the flesh. Bonnie meets with a young girl in dire straits, scared of the life that grows in her womb and leads her to Truth. This young woman is seen and known and not on her own — now.

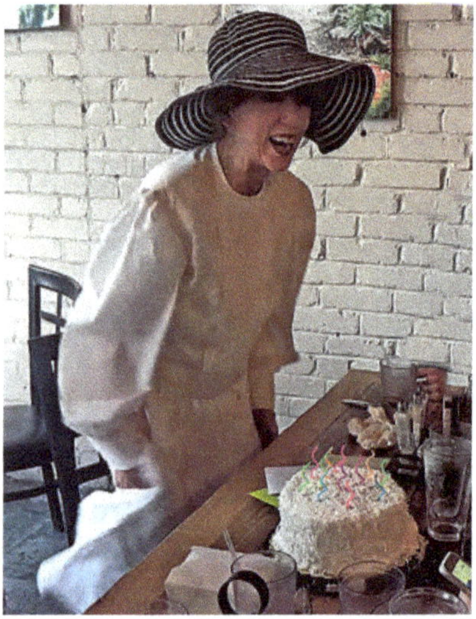

Then there's a place south of town where guards work 24/7. Local folks are on edge about the tall fence with barbed wire and even more on edge about the men who live there. But not Bonnie. It takes some time for the guards to pat her down. (Do you think they check her nest of hair?) Once they're done, Bonnie walks in and talks about being free in Jesus — this to men who every day see only metal bars and a gray slab.

Now, don't be fooled. Bonnie's search to share Jesus doesn't end at the edge of her town. Every June, she flies to Mexico and stays in a home full of kids who lack a mom or dad. I've seen a photo or two. The faces around her beam with real joy; they know God's love through her.

If you ever have the chance to meet Bonnie, you'll need to yell when you talk to her; she can't hear as well as she used to. But she won't raise her voice in reply. Even though her words of love are soft, they're strong and firm.

With no thought of the world's rash view of her, she keeps on.

"Jesus loves you," Bonnie says. Only when each guy and gal, young and old, knows this hope will she slip off her boots, let those feet breathe, and then lay down to rest.

39

My Long-Haired Hippie Liar

Marcella Ruch

He stood at the front of the room, looking totally out of place. He was clean shaven, but his clothes lacked care in both choosing and handling. His hair hung straggly over his collar. It was dark, like his eyes. The social director read from the card he had filled out at the door of the Parents Without Partners (PWP) meeting. I barely heard what he said since I had long ago given up on men. They all seemed to care about only one thing, and it wasn't the welfare of me or my four children. After I heard the word "philosophy," I was all ears. Just out of high school, I had gone to Moody Bible Institute summer school and loved to study theology. The social director read on: "Sports: soccer, basketball, football, Frisbee, hiking, camping, and backpacking; Books: novels, non-fiction, poetry, biography, and history; Music: classical, opera, folk, musicals, and singing." Now I was stopped cold; I hung on every word. I loved all of the above and my four kids and I loved to hike in our Colorado mountains. His last line before they both sat down was: "Employment: mathematician working as a computer programmer for the Air Force at NORAD."

Looking at him more closely, I began to think that the look on his face must really be guilt for lying about all those interests and his place of work. Also, I saw that he was too young for me. My husband and I had divorced three years before. My mom was living with me while I completed an internship at Pikes Peak Community College. After I got home that night, she had pounced on me, saying, "Get dressed up, Young Lady, You are going out!" I had no idea where to go since I didn't go to bars. I was a member of PWP but had stopped attending their meetings, except children's activities. "I don't like the way you live, Marcella Joyce," Mom went on. "All you do is work, come home take care of your kids, do the laundry, clean house, work in your yard, do your homework, and then start all over again the next week. That's no way for a young woman to live!" Most of the time my mom was proud of me; I sure wasn't used to her chewing me out. So I called a few caring single-mother friends to go to PWP with me.

The more I thought about this young man, the more I thought that maybe we could be friends. I would love a friend with whom I could discuss ideas, books, music, and maybe even poetry. Later I told one of the women in the ladies' room that I'd like to meet "the new guy."

As soon as the group of us ladies went upstairs for punch and sweets, the woman from the restroom grabbed my arm and the arm of the new guy, pulling him toward me and saying, "This lady would like to meet you!"

I was shocked, and he seemed to feel the same. But still I was able to think of one thing to say: "Did you make up all that stuff they read off of the card up front, or is it the truth?"

He looked at me and —blushing— said, "Why do you ask?"

"Because they said you were interested in philosophy. Are you interested in philosophy?"

"Well, yes, a particular branch; it is called theology." And on that note, we began a conversation. He learned that I had one friend, a Catholic priest, with whom I had lunch now and then to talk theology. I learned that he was highly articulate, with a keen gaze. Before we parted, we found that we were both reading the same book: Abraham Maslow's *The Farther Reaches of Human Nature*. We did not learn each other's names or phone numbers, and though I still thought he could end up being a friend, I feared I would never hear from him — even though I very much wanted to. He was the most interesting man I had spoken to in the three years I had been single.

Several times over the weekend, the new guy from PWP, Pete Ruch, contacted his friend, the secretary of PWP and finally convinced her to break the rules and give him my phone number. Later, during our "date" at Denny's, I learned that he had three boys, one of whom was the same age as my fourteen-year-old son. His wife had left him for another man. He had been divorced three years followed by a few failed attempts to try to restart the marriage. He had chosen not to date so he could focus on his sons.

His brother had convinced him that night to get out of the house and meet people. We agreed to meet for lunch each day that next week. At lunch, he would read me poetry in between conversations. In a few months the poetry he was reading was love sonnets. He was younger by a year and three months. But he was intelligent. He did not cheat on his wife. He was paying full child support even though he was raising the boys because she was working on getting her PhD. He was not mad at this ex-wife, just sad that he had not been able to make her happy.

We had lunch together every day until summer when we began to add weekend picnics and camping with all seven children. We didn't know where all this would go but really enjoyed being with each other and seemed to be falling in love, more so every month. But then, on Labor Day weekend, Pete got a call from his ex-wife who wanted him to come back to her to try to keep the family intact for the sake of the children.

Both devastated, Pete and I also agreed that it was the right thing to do. Days later, after I went home from the hospital after eye surgery, Pete called me. He asked if he could come over. It was September 17th. He came in, full of delight to see me, even though I was still a mess. The cast on my face made me look like a racoon. He didn't seem to mind. He came into my room and knelt on one knee. "I love you," he said. Will you marry me?"

"Yes, yes, yes!"

On my September 20th birthday, Pete arrived with a stack of birthday presents that seemed a mile high. On his visit the next day he had to admit, "I went overboard for your birthday and spent too much money. I want to buy you the world, but I can't afford it. What do you think about us not buying each other presents, but instead writing poems to each other for special occasions?" So, that is what we have been doing for 45 years.

We had one important difference to work out. I was a bit of a workaholic, and he loved to play. He played soccer with a team in the city. He played ball every afternoon with his boys. He read about 20 books a week. That didn't leave much time for house chores. We worked out a trade off: If I would let him teach me how to play, he would let me teach him how to work.

Then there was that long hair. He refused to waste money on a barber but agreed that I could cut his hair. Gradually we worked up to a normal man's haircut. I had to learn how to cut hair, but Pete was patient. To this day, he has never been to a barber.

Early on December 20-second that first year, Pete took me to the mountains. There, we walked up a steep slope to a pristine blue lake where we said our private vows to each other. We promised to love and care for each other's children and for each other's elderly widowed mothers. We pledged our love forever in God's green forest by that beautiful lake. Then we drove back down to make our pledges legal at the church later that afternoon.

That night and for the next few nights, Pete cried about not being in the same house with his boys. It was so hard to give the boys back to their mother after three years. I just held him close while he cried. He was never sorry we wed but sad to move out away from his boys. After a short time, they would spend three nights a week at our new house, and when they were in their own home, he would go and tuck them into bed and then come back.

On our first Christmas, I told Pete to invite his former wife and her new husband for Christmas Dinner. That began a tradition that lasted for over 40 years — until we moved to Florida. Despite the boys' marrying and having their own families, we were together for every holiday and birthday and any other special occasions. This included our 45th wedding anniversary party in December of 2018.

After we had been married five years, we adopted a five-year-old-boy. He was a delightful-but-troubled child, as he bore the scars of being given up. We loved him and raised him the best we could. Today he credits our love with being the only thing that kept him alive during his teen years. He grew to be a wonderful man, and all our seven are adults, comfortable in their own skin, and capable of love for another person. They have given us nine grandchildren and six great-grand-children. Our children tease us about being love birds.

About the title, "My Long-haired Hippie Liar" — Pete did try being a hippie but found out that it is a scary world out there, so he didn't want to be a hippie after all. As for the lying, after I had come to know Pete well, I learned that he is one of the most truthful people on the face of the earth. It wasn't guilt that I had read on his face that first night. He was just embarrassed standing up in front at PWP since he'd thought that what he'd put on that card would just be fed into a computer. But I'm really glad it was read out loud. Only in that way was I able to get a glimpse of the real Peter: my love, now and forever. We still write each other love poems.

Pete claims to be a success in that he has taught me well how to play. But he claims that I failed, in that he never learned how to work. I say that I succeeded in that he retired only after all of 31 years with the Air Force. He is still learning to work — even after his 80th birthday when he began to use his new electric drill/screwdriver.

For my part, I am learning to ride the three-wheel bike that he bought me.

So you see, we both won. He has learned how to work, and I have learned how to play. Both of us have learned how to love.

40

An Original Thirty-Something

Jeanie Connell

Meet Libby, a 30-something who looks 20. Her long dark hair, pretty face, and style of dress speak with no words. In fact, if she doesn't know you, her words are few. When she does speak, though, her words are choice, many, and fast-paced. Through the pitch and tone of her voice, she takes the lead in conversation. She has a gift with her speech that leaves no doubt in the minds of those who hear her as to what is *her way* and *her why*. Libby's trademark quotes are, "True Dat," "Don't nobody care about your ______, " and "I just can't." What she can do is join small words like macaroni on a string in a way that kids who hear will want to copy her each time. Her "Oh no, Buddy Row," always brings a smile.

She lights up a room with no desire to be the center of it. Her goal is to help others find *their* identity. "Tha's you, ain't it?" is Libby's way of saying, "You be you, and I'll be me."

That she never likes to be the star, the one to stand out, may be why she never played sports. Now, she can name every score, every athlete, and all the stats from basketball and golf to soccer and football.

Over the span of her career Libby has been a nanny to three families. With each she has been tough and kind and means what she says. She may seem bossy, but in her role she needs to be direct. Her job is about family. She is the glue that holds them fast to each other. Her choice not to have a child of her own has given her the chance to love, teach, and train the children of others.

Her *first* family is her husband of seven years, Erik, and their dog, Watson, with whom she lives in their seven-room place in Atlanta. Each of the years they've been wed, they have gone to Las Vegas to renew their vows and shop.

Libby's family also includes the mother and father God gave her and the two brothers she grew up with. Both siblings thank God for her each day. If they need help, Libby is the one they call. They will ask her what she thinks in most things and laugh with her about sports, quotes, and kids.

She gets it! She lives with zest and has a spark that others can only hope for. She asks you in and you know she cares. Libby shines with get-up-and-go. No wonder her niece and nephews adore her. Over and over in the past eight years, Libby has gone to their ball games and shared every birthday. Her creativity is off the charts and helps her to choose just the right gift that each family member would love.

Unlike high school, college well fit her style of learning. While there, she saw each subject through the lens she loved: clothes, shoes, and trends. In some ways, she was her own instructor. As she went after her degree in fashion design, her education was to wear it, stick with her choice, and only then check the label. Still, she made it a point to know each designer from Kate Spade to Tommy Hilfiger.

Ever since Libby was a small child, her choices have been hers alone, and from that time on she has had a true sense of the look she was going for. Friends and family would always copy her. Even though she has two closets full of clothes, she lives most days in yoga pants, a tee shirt, and tennis shoes — while pulling back her long curls into a ponytail.

Libby owns more than 100 pairs of Nike brand shoes. I couldn't count the times others have stopped her to ask where she'd found such a cute pair. She has come close to the label shopaholic, yet she has given away more than she owns. Kind is her true label — kind to everyone. This 30-something is color blind. Her eyes see no black race or white race but just one race, the human race.

Her boss pays her extra to clean and in other ways run their home. Since part of her job is to drive their son an hour to school and back each day, the parents have given her two cars, each a Lexus. (One came with a red bow) They love to *say* thank you, and Libby loves to *hear* thank you. They have also blessed her by putting braces on her teeth — way overdue for a 30-something.

Until Libby came, they never ate a home-cooked meal. Now they clamor for the food she makes, since they have been able to try it and to know they like it. Her own home can look messed and stressed, but she keeps the home where she works neat as a pin.

Some would think Libby harsh when she speaks to me in a voice that seems less than kind. What they don't know is her passion for integrity. She knows me more than most do, and I don't regret her honesty even if it seems sharp at times.

When I knew her as a teen I didn't like her, nor did I trust her. Now, the Libby at 30-something is a best friend. Once a year, we go to New York City to shop and to thank God for our roles as mother and daughter.

41

A Sure Thing

Kim Wilch

Some kids have grandmas who rock in chairs. My grandma rocked, for sure — just not in a chair. She gave with her whole heart, even when she didn't have much. She was there for me, day in and day out. Grandma taught me to be silly and have fun. "Life is short," was her motto, and she coaxed me to take risks.

She was happy in 'most all that she did — but even more so if there was a way to bet on it.

On Saturday nights my sister and I stayed over at Grandma's house, just five blocks away. First, we played cards with the aunts — games like Kings in the Corner, Crazy Eights, or Pokeno. We played for a penny a card when we were six and ten years old. On a lucky night, we cashed out for 25 cents. We laughed until tears spilled down our cheeks.

After the stand up, sit down, church drill on Sunday morning, we went to a local donut shop. With a gleam in her eye, Grandma shared our next stop. In the summer, her leap of faith led us to a church fair. She didn't care where it was or how far away; we made the trek. As we dashed to the action, she gave us money to play "games of chance" ('though we kids would joke that it took *skill* to win). We tossed small rings onto two-liter jugs of pop and cast ping pong balls into fish bowls.

We'd find Grandma at the meat wheel. When the wheel slowed and the arrow came close to one of grandma's wins, sparks danced in her eyes and she got fired up. What a thrill! When the wheel stopped on her wedge, she would win a slab of bacon, a ham, or salami. We couldn't go home until she won all three. Lucky us.

At her own church fair, Grandma was in charge of the cake walk. She longed for each risk taker to win. If you sat next to the lucky champ, you'd get a plate of cookies. Bless her heart.

One day, my sister and I went to her with an idea to raise money for the Muscular Dystrophy Telethon. Grandma clapped, "Let's put on a carnival of our own!"

"That's a fantastic idea!" we cheered.

Mom helped make signs to hype the event, and dad taught us how to build booths. Grandma was on prize duty and called friends to bake cakes and run the games. The neighborhood kids had a blast at the duck pond, tic-tac-toe bean-bag toss, and our very own cake walk. Pride surged when we took the loot to a local site to make our pledge. Our hard work had paid off. Grandma taught us that kids can help too.

When it came to scratch cards, pull tabs, and World Series pools; Grandma was also all in. At the horse track, she would wager her age on the Daily Double. When I turned 12, I was of age to go to the bingo hall in the next state. Pride beamed from her eyes as I yelled, "Bingo!" when I-26 was called. Even though she had paid my way, she let me keep the prize money.

Once when she bet on football, Grandma urged me to stake ten bucks on the Chicago Bears since it was a sure thing. I let out my breath when they won; that was too rich for my young blood.

Catherine Prerost

As we moved her from her home, my son sat on the sofa she'd left behind. "Mom, what was that? Did you hear a noise?" He raised the seat to find sports info and point-spread sheets.

Oh, Granny!

Slots were Granny's top choice. On a jaunt to Nevada, she and I were down to our last coins with a few hours until the bus would take us to the plane. I thought we should play penny slots to stretch out our play time. She gave me the thumbs down. "Poo on that," she said with a flick of her wrist. "We're betting dollars." We took turns as we plunked a token into the slot. She balked at me when I rubbed its belly for good luck or took too long on my turn. At her pace, we would be out of money in five ticks. Soon, the slot began to spew coins. This upset her since she couldn't play while it paid out. She moved on to the next gizmo, and I cleaned up the loot in her wake. Calm swept over me as we got back to even, as chance would have it, just in time for the bus to leave. (I have never gained her nerves of steel.)

As she got older and began to fail, I called daily to check on her. "Hi, Grandma! What are you up to today?"

"Huh?"

"What did you have for breakfast?"

"Huh? "

"Would you like to go to the casino?"

"What time will you pick me up?"

"Oh Granny, you crack me up!" On the way, heaven help us if the light stayed red too long. With a wink of her eye and a snap of her wrist, she urged me to run the light — as if the slots had begun to call her name.

Some say she was lucky. In truth, I was the one who hit it big to have her for a grandmother. Until the day she died at the age of 94, she never lost her love of the games. She was laid to rest in her prized red shirt. It had a slot scene on the front, three sevens in a row, and lights that blinked. Even though Grandma was a fun lover, we left the switch off, so people weren't too shocked. She held a slot token while prayer beads draped her hands. With a laugh in my soul, I could see her place a bet on who would get their angel wings next.

About the Authors

"Adventure," "ambition," and "attitude" are **Becky Alexander**'s (p. 41) three favorite words. She leads tours to Washington DC, New York City, Toronto, Niagara Falls, and other destinations. Before her travel adventures, she taught kids about Jesus for 25 years as a children's minister. She has been published over 70 times, including magazine articles for Parent Life, Experiencing God, Special Education Today, The Minister's Family, Pockets, Christian Living in the Mature Years, and The Lutheran Digest.

Becky was born with one arm and has worn a prosthetic arm since she was one year old. You can read about her experiences in her book, *One Smile, One Arm*, and online at www.onesmileonearm.com. She and her husband live in Alabama and have two adult children and one granddaughter.

Karen O'Kelley Allen (p. 14) has a passion for music, ministry, and dogs. Recently retired from working in cancer research at the University of Alabama Comprehensive Cancer Center, she plans to fill her time with more writing, more exercise, more travel, and more mission work. She still enjoys her part-time job playing the organ for Meadow Brook Baptist in Birmingham, Alabama where she and her husband of 36 years, George Parker (Parky), attend.

A diagnosis of breast cancer inspired her to write her Bible study *Confronting Cancer with Faith*, which has brought encouragement to readers around the world.

Karen enjoys speaking, singing, and writing and has published numerous articles and devotionals through LifeWay Christian Resources, Grace Publishing, The Alabama Baptist newspaper, and other Christian magazines.

Mary Alice Archer (p. 60) has worked in education for over 40 years. For the last 25 years she has taught middle schoolers a variety of subjects including math, English, history, French, art, drama, and science. She has a B.S. in Exceptional Education from the University of Central Florida.

Mary Alice has written and illustrated an award-winning children's book, *If a Cat.*

She and her husband, John, have performed in Christian theater for many years and are now creating a YouTube series with their grandchildren on little known facts about Benjamin Franklin called, *Ben There, Done That!*

A Southern California girl for the first 40 years of her life, she now lives in Central Florida. She and John have three children, six grandchildren, two dogs, a lovebird, and a Hermann's tortoise named Mel.

Lanita Bradley Boyd (p. 31), a freelance writer and speaker, draws on years of teaching, church ministry, and family experiences in her writing. She enjoys mentoring young women through Bible studies and planning spiritually uplifting events.

Lanita travels with her family and has been on mission trips lasting three to six weeks each. On these trips to Brazil, Panama, Fiji, Malaysia, and Thailand, she offers free English lessons based on Bible stories and works locally to help new English speakers improve their language skills.

Lanita is married to Stephen Boyd — speaker, author, and minister. They live in Fort Thomas, Kentucky, a suburb of Cincinnati, Ohio, where they serve at the Central Church of Christ. They have a son and daughter who brought to the family another daughter and son and four wonderful grandchildren. She can be reached at lanitaboyd@gmail.com.

Nancy Brashear, Ph.D. (p. 100), wrote her first poem (about sitting in the fog on a bench with magical creatures swirling around her) when she was eight years old. She's been composing poetry and prose ever since. As an adult, she has published several short stories and poems and has written three unpublished (so far!) novels.

She is Professor Emeritus from Azusa Pacific University, has written articles and chapters for academic books, regularly writes blog reviews for The International Literacy Association (for children's and adolescent literature), and has participated in poetry and short story readings.

Nancy met her husband when they were in the eighth grade. She's the proud grandmother of seven talented, independent young girls (some of whom are already budding writers), ranging in age from three to eleven.

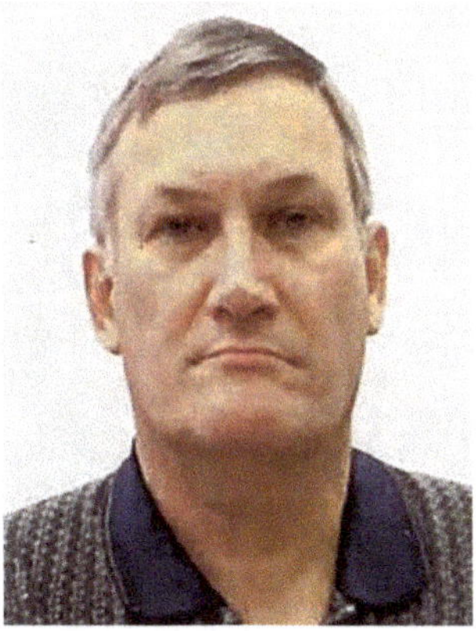

David Buster (p. 95) has found it easier to figure out most diagnoses over his 40 years in medicine than to decide what to do after retiring from that career. He is glad to be able to treat things around the yard and home that missed appointments with him during those working years. Getting up late allows him to stay up late to finish a good movie. A cat lands on his lap when it knows he needs a nap.

His guitar gathers dust waiting in the line behind the chores and health issues that he has found to bug people his age.

The demands of 3 A.M. ideas have replaced early morning calls to assist in surgery. Training those ideas to pull together as a team usually keeps him up well after sunrise. Feed the ideas. Feed the cats. Then off to bed instead of the office.

He has started to discern a routine in there somewhere.

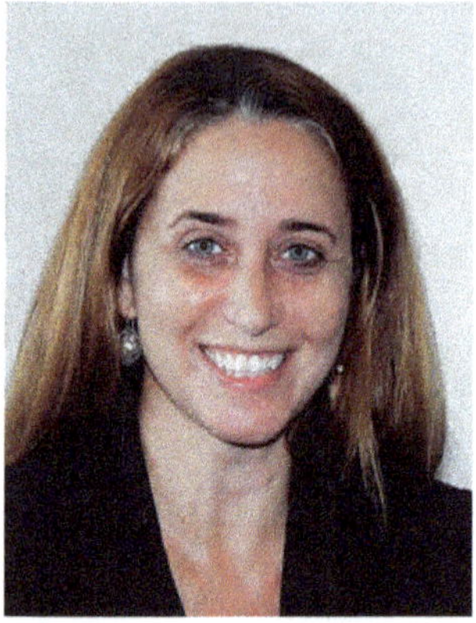

Julie Ann Chase (p. 39), a Dean at Southern Maine Community College, lives on the coast of Maine. The blogger (www.mugupmermaid.com) and aspiring author, caught the writing bug as a child when she won a contest and got to meet *Newberry* medalist, William Armstrong.

She is active in her community, serving on nonprofit boards, volunteering time with her church, and helping lead various leadership and spiritual retreats. She loves to be in, on, or near water, preferably the ocean. Her home is full of hair from her three rescue dogs, but even more full with love.

Diagnosed with breast cancer in 2017, she has been overwhelmed by the love of her family, friends, co-workers, church, and even complete strangers. Julie credits Lin Daniels for encouraging her to tackle the challenge for this book while undergoing neurocognitive therapy.

Jeanie Connell (p. 113) was born in Michigan, graduated from high school in Illinois and attended college nearby where she met Michael, her husband of 48 years. Married life began in Ohio and included several other states until their recent move to Franklin, Tennessee.

They have three children who inspired Jeanie's first book, *All I Needed to Know About Being a Grown-Up, I Learned from My Kids.*

She recorded *All I Have to Share*, her first CD of original songs, in 1986. Her second CD, *Roots*, offered songs of hope reflecting ten years of recovery. In 2007 Jeanie recorded, *I Call His Name,* which led to her first book of poetry, *God's HeartStrings*.

She has published devotions in *One Step at a Time* and *Seasons of a Woman's Heart.*

Dennis Conrad (p. 28) writes inspirational fiction. He is a retired public-speaker and English professor who taught at Barstow Community College (BCC) in California. As part of his responsibility with BCC, Dennis taught seven years at Fort Irwin, the National Training Center for the United States Army. He also taught speech and English five summers in Kazakhstan, Central Asia, two summers in South Korea, and three summers in China.

Dennis has been married to Diane 29 years, and she is his editor. They enjoy time with family, taking daily walks around a lake and traveling. Both active in church, Dennis is also in a men's group. He serves on the Board of Directors of Diamond Valley Writers' Guild in Hemet, California.

Bonnie Culp (p. 17) is a recently retired high school teacher who lives in Southern California. She and her late husband raised two daughters, who have married and started families. They have blessed her with five busy and energetic grandchildren who keep everyone going.

Bonnie has a masters degree in child development and taught in the public schools for 25 years. She also has taught in children's ministry for over 40 years.

She recently published her first children's book, *Little Is Much When God Is in It,* and she is currently working on a children's devotional series by the same title.

For fun she likes to golf, paint, garden, and travel. She also dabbles in furniture restoration. She considers herself a jack of all trades but master of none.

After 40 years, **Lin Daniels** (p. 67) retired from teaching physical education — all but one year serving at the elementary-school level. She and her twin sister are avid golfers and especially enjoy playing as partners. As such they negotiate over which identical clothing to wear but choose one item (usually a hat) to be different. It is essential to zig and zag as teammates, so they have to remain slightly dissimilar.

Recently, Lin has found a passion for pickleball — a game similar to tennis but played on a smaller court while using a whiffle ball. Her other interests include writing Christian devotions, working with youth at church, and preaching — when offered the opportunity. Lin gives thanks to God for the depths of His love as well as all the "surprises" He has graciously bestowed on her.

Jorja Davis (p. 51) learned a lot from her daddy. Probably most important was facing life with courage and faith. She spent 26 years as an Air Force wife. Her children always told others she was "mom to half the free world." She and her husband of 50 years have two home-grown daughters, three home-grown grandchildren, and more collected children, grandchildren and great-grandchildren than they can count.

Always a teacher, like both her parents, she chased her certification around the world and across ages and fields. Jorja is currently retired, teaches piano, and researches and teaches a weekly drop-in Bible study on the Revised Common Lectionary. The deeper she goes and the higher she flies, the more she learns that everything God asks her to do "should make her a little bit afraid."

Retired elementary school principal **Nicey T. Eller** (p. 97) traded professional suits for cowgirl boots when she and her husband, Jay, moved to the country to build a log home, raise cattle, and enjoy more time with their children and grandchildren.

An author, poet, and prolific letter writer, Nicey remains active in education as a mentor and consultant. She serves in her church as a teacher and Celebrate Recovery leader. She relishes brisk walks and has completed two half-marathon trail races, actually finishing before a few runners who were not injured. Her favorite sound is laughter born of joy and triumph. Of all her blessings, she is most grateful for grace.

Nicey and Jay, loyal Troy University Trojan sports fans, live in Abbeville, Alabama.

Like her aunt's life in the story, "Being Jackie," **Pam Grove**'s (p. 36) life has strayed a bit from the norm. After college she moved from Portland, Oregon to teach school in an isolated rural town. She married fellow teacher, Stan, three months after they met. When their family grew to six adopted children, she chose a new role: stay-at-home mom.

Writing has been a part of her life since elementary school. She says it has been a fun learning experience writing for *Short and Sweet* including, building skills in choosing the best word and cutting what does not move the story forward. Pam's husband passed away from a rare form of cancer, microcystic adnexal carcinoma, at age 62. Through it all they took joy in their family and always trusted that God was with them. GrovesWords@gmail.com

Leah "LM" Hinton (p. 92) always has her nose in a book, whether she is reading it or writing it. She and her two children (and five dogs) keep house in Dallas, Texas. She spends her days in cafes where she drinks far too much coffee while pouring words onto the page writing fiction, non-fiction, poetry, and her latest love, stage plays, which have been featured at prominent festivals throughout Texas.

Besides highly caffeinated coffee, Leah is fueled by a never-ending faith in God. A country girl at heart, this homeschool mom loves sharing her struggles and blessings with others going through similar situations and firmly believes that faith is the best remedy for life's toils. Find her at AuthorLMHinton.com and on Twitter, Instagram and Facebook @ AuthorLMHinton.

Patricia Huey (p. 11) was born in the Pacific Northwest but raised in the South. She began her teaching career soon after graduating from the University of Alabama. Throughout her career, the subject she most enjoyed teaching was creative writing. In 2015, she retired as director of Hill Creek Christian School in Mount Vernon, Washington, the school she founded in 1994.

These days, she serves on the Hill Creek Board of Directors.

Currently, in addition to short, inspirational pieces, Patricia is writing a memoir about starting Hill Creek and the insights she gained. In her spare time, she enjoys spending time with family, friends, and her two Labrador retrievers, Braveheart and Scout.

Award-winning author, speaker and blogger, **Penny L. Hunt** (p. 48) enjoys writing for both children and adults. Her writing has appeared in *Chicken Soup for the Soul*, *Guideposts*, *The Upper Room*, almost every edition of the *Short and Sweet* series, and on-line in *Just 18 Summers*. Her most recent book, *Bounce! Don't Break...* helps others bounce back quicker from setbacks. *Little White Squirrel's Secret-A Special Place to Practice*, is an Amazon.com bestseller children's book dedicated to her severely autistic granddaughter.

Living in the rural peach growing region of South Carolina with her husband Bill, a retired career naval officer and attaché, and their two dogs, Penny enjoys gardening and gourmet cooking. Her greatest passion is to lead others to a personal and intimate relationship with Christ. Visit her at PennyLHunt.com.

Liz Kimmel (p. 45) lives in St. Paul Minnesota, has been married for 40 years, is mother to two and grandmother to four. She earned a BA in Elementary Education at Bethel College in Arden Hills, Minnesota.

She has published two books of Christian prose/poetry and a grammar workbook for middle-school students.

Her current projects include a series of picture books which will help children understand God's nature through nature, and a workbook of activity sheets about all 50 States. Several of her devotions will be included in the 2020 Guideposts book *All God's Creatures*. She is Communications Coordinator for her St. Paul church, where she writes and is the layout editor for a bi-monthly publication whose purpose is to inspire, strengthen, and edify the congregation and beyond.

Rachel Lulich (p. 19) is a writer and freelance developmental editor with Broken Top Editing. Rachel has been published in *Clarinet News* magazine and was twice featured as a guest blogger on singer/songwriter Ginny Owens' website. She has self-published a poetry collection titled *To Do This Right: Poems of Faith.* Her first original stage play, about the Confessing Church in 1930s Germany, was performed at Lake Bible Church in 2018. Her debut novel, *Random Walk,* will launch in December 2019.

Born and raised in the Pacific Northwest, she recently moved to Slovakia to teach English. When she's not writing, editing or teaching, Rachel loves to read, sing, and travel.

Author **Terry Magness** (p. 82) loves people and their stories. An amazing account of a simple man who, as an abused give-away child, learned to know God, overcame his personal challenges, and was mightily used of Him, is featured in her book, *Azadiah Reynolds-God's Jamaica Man.*

In order to help people know the heart of God and to grow personally and in their relationship with the Lord, she established a Biblically based teaching and discipleship ministry called Grace Harbour.

As an ordained minister and pastoral counselor, she currently serves to undergird pastors, their wives, and others serving God in ministry. Her writings and local church classes are directed toward encouraging and empowering the body of Christ.

She and her husband, Don, live near Springfield, Missouri and have two adult children and three beautiful granddaughters.

Jill Allen Maisch (p. 90) lives in Maryland with her pastor husband, Bill. They are blessed to live close to her mom and within a short drive of all six of their adult children and their families. Being MomMom and PopPop to their grandchildren brings them much joy. When they're not working, Bill and she enjoy traveling, camping in their RV, and flying in their small, private plane.

While she enjoys teaching middle school science in their community, her passion is leading cross-cultural-mission experiences. Most summers since 2006 she has been leading teams that serve among the Hopi people in Northeast Arizona.

Fairly recently she has discovered a love of writing devotions and essays. Several devotions have already been published in *The Upper Room* and this is her third contribution to the *Short and Sweet* series.

Cristina Moore (p. 34) was born in Puerto Rico and grew up in Tennessee. She currently lives in North Carolina with her husband of over 20 years and her 4 children; Tripp (27), Katie (24), Hope (9) and Helena (9). She is the owner and CEO of Bronze Star Homes, an employee at Duke Energy, and currently serves in the North Carolina National Guard as a Brigade Commander of the 130th Maneuver Enhancement Brigade.

Cristina celebrates God's Word by sharing the grace and miracles both she and her husband have witnessed through multiple combat deployments and their call to serve their community and country.

In her spare time, she places family as a priority and is enjoying returning to her passion of writing and touching the lives of those reading her work.

Alice H. Murray (p. 85) is an adoption attorney who has practiced law in Florida for 30 years. While being a lawyer is her profession, Alice's passion is writing. She is a staff writer for www.adoption.com, has had pieces published in four *Short and Sweet* books and in *Chicken Soup for the Soul*, and has written for legal professional magazines, her local paper, a missions magazine, and various online sites.

Alice is an officer and board member of the Florida Adoption Council and of Hope Global Initiative. She hopes to have two books published in the near future — one a humorous devotional book and one a look back at her career as "Boss of the Babies" doing adoption work.

Before his retirement as a United Methodist minister, **Tony R. Nester** (p. 74) pastored churches in New Jersey and Iowa, including Des Moines, Council Bluffs, and Sioux City. Currently, Tony continues his preaching ministry as an occasional supply pastor. He earned theological degrees from Princeton Theological Seminary and the University of Dubuque Theological Seminary and is a former adjunct professor at Morningside College in Sioux City, Iowa.

Tony currently resides in Urbandale, Iowa. He is married and a father to three grown children and grandfather to eight grandchildren.

He has a special love for spending time in the Sangre de Cristo mountain area of Colorado. He enjoys writing and reading — especially the works of C. S. Lewis.

Shelley Pierce (p. 63) and her husband, James, live in the mountains of east Tennessee where he pastors Towering Oaks Baptist Church. She serves alongside him on staff as Director of Preschool and Children's Ministries. They raised four children and now enjoy the gift of grandchildren.

She is an award-winning author of the middle-grade series *The Crumberry Chronicles* (*The Wish I Wished Last Night* & *Battle Buddies*), *Sweet Moments: Insight and Encouragement for the Pastor's Wife* and has contributed to numerous books and devotional works including *The Upper Room* magazine, *Power for Living*, and *Guidepost Christmas Edition*. In June 2019, she released her first picture book, *I Know What Grandma Does While I'm Napping*. Her current work in progress is volume three in *The Crumberry Chronicles*.

Surrounded by fossils, relics, and crusty antiques, **Ken Proctor** (p. 102) works from his home in Vancouver, Washington. His cramped little office resembles a museum's back storeroom.

"From the Shadows" is Ken's second contribution to the *Short and Sweet* series. (See "Angel Falls" in *Short and Sweet Takes the Fifth*.) Another humorous short story, "Crawl," will appear in the next issue of *Timberline Review*, joining several how-to articles appearing in *Countryside* magazine. These all fall outside Ken's usual genre of historical fiction (featured at kenproctorauthor.com), but so do his current projects: a "Hallmarky" Christmas romantic comedy and a suspense/thriller set on the Oregon Coast.

Reba Rhyne (p. 77) is the pen name of Reba Carolyn Rhyne Meiller, whose writing is influenced by her southern roots in the western foothills of the Great Smoky Mountains. As a consultant to the marine industry, she prototyped upholstered interiors for major boat manufacturers from Texas to North Carolina.

Believing that a writer should experience the setting of her work, she spends time in the area she writes about — giving the story the authentic quality she craves.

In her *Tipton Chronicles* series of three Christian-oriented novels — *Butterfield Station, Chilhowee Legacy,* and *My Cherokee Rose* — Reba uses historical facts and places associated with her ancestors.

As a Christ-follower for 60 years, she believes her responsibility is to follow the Great Commission found in Matthew. She may be contacted at rebarhyne@gmail.com.

After graduating from local schools and the University of Redlands, **Susanna Robar** (p. 54) married Robert, now retired as a Los Angeles City fire captain. He and Susanna, a retired Spanish teacher, have five children: two children are with the Lord; three adult children and four grandchildren live in Southern California.

Through Susanna Robar Ministries — RapeSpeaksOut! — Susanna uses written materials, workshops, seminars, and short-term courses to educate parents, teachers, pastors, and other child caregivers about sexual violence, child safety, and human-sex trafficking. Her purpose is to help heal victims of sexual violence and prevent more children from becoming such victims.

For her efforts, Susanna received the Inaugural Cottey College Alumnae Hall of Leadership and Social Responsibility Award.

Marcella Rejoice Ruch (p. 107), Ph.D. is a retired teacher/administrator who was called to heal the sick while on a mission trip to Russia. As a result, along with 40 volunteers from Sunrise UMC in Colorado Springs, she started a free medical clinic now called "Mission Center." She also started a free pharmacy called "The Lord Cares Pharmacy" and a ministry In Kakata, Liberia called Healthy Women, Healthy Liberia. She currently teaches a Cancer Survivor's Cooking Class. Marcella and Peter had their children in their first marriages: Peter's three boys and Marcella's three girls and one boy. After five years together, they adopted a five-year-old-boy.

With nine grandchildren and seven great-grandchildren, Marcella's and Peter's life in Florida is rich in love as they help raise an eight-year-old great-grand-daughter and babysit a new baby two days a week.

Michelle Ruschman (p. 80) lives on the Florida panhandle with her husband, Mark, and their daughter. Michelle writes primarily as a way of expressing her faith and to help her make sense of a confusing world. She recently joined the writing team for *GO!*, a Christian magazine, to write devotions and feature articles for their Emerald Coast edition.

During the times her words don't come so easily, art is her other language. She works mainly in alcohol inks, acrylic paint, and mixed media. Her work has been shown in the Pensacola Museum of Art, and she has been a featured artist in their local library. Since 2008, she has been a jewelry artisan using native Philippine wood beads, metal, and fused glass. She is most known for Beautifully Broken, her line of dichroic glass crosses.

From her start in Michigan to her current home in Arizona, **Cybele Sieradzki** (p. 43) has lived in 27 homes in eight states. Her interest in creative writing emerged while she worked on her B.A. in English at Maryville College in Tennessee. She discovered New Directions publications in the back corner of the Gateway Bookstore in Knoxville and wanted to be a Beatnik and write poetry like Lawrence Ferlinghetti and ee cummings. Instead, she married a space engineer then acquired an M.A. in Experimental Psychology.

After eons in technical writing and editing and a brief second career in social-services-program evaluations, Cybele returned to her true passion. At home at last in the desert, she finds her creative energies flowing again and spends as much time as possible writing memoir and essays.

Dubbed "The Parable Teacher," long-time Bible student and teacher **Lisa Worthey Smith** (p. 65) often uses simple things in nature to point to truths in the Word of God.

For years, God prompted the subject of her piece, Thanh Boyer, to write down her life story to encourage more people in their struggles. Because English was not Thanh's first language, she asked God to send her an author. After reading Lisa's *The Wisdom Tree*, Thanh contacted her. Together, they penned *The Ground Kisser* and dedicated it to God and the US military, especially the Vietnam veterans. It released in 2019.

Lisa and her husband are empty nesting in northern Alabama where she spends time in her backyard oasis, which includes a hummingbird garden for Oscar The Extraordinary Hummingbird, where she gathers inspiration to write stories of faith hope and love.

Judee Stapp (p. 20) is a popular speaker for Stonecroft Ministries, retreats, and other women's events. She uses her engaging style and humorous life experiences to inspire women to strengthen their faith and find their purpose.

Her stories and poems have been published in several magazines and many *Chicken Soup for the Soul* books. She is currently working on a children's book and an anthology of first-person stories that encourage women to live with true joy.

Judee lives in Placentia, California with her husband John. They have a daughter, son-in-law, and three grandchildren in Minnesota; a son in Pittsburg; and a daughter, son-in-law, and three-year-old grandson in Murietta, California. Judee is President of the Angel Baseball Booster Club and enjoys scrapbooking, theater, and church activities.

For over 30 years, fourth-generation-native Nashvillian **Marilyn Switzer** (p. 87) has led walking tours of downtown Nashville for school students studying Tennessee history. She has been married for 45 years to Ken, Chief Judge for the Tennessee Workers' Compensation Court of Claims. They are the parents of two children and the grandparents of two grandsons — Simeon and Max — and a granddaughter, Violet.

When not working or hosting little folks for playdates with Mellie (their name for Marilyn), she enjoys dabbling in a bit of writing in a blog, participating in photo challenges on Facebook, hosting small dinner parties, making watercolor greeting cards for family and friends, and crafting — especially if it involves small explosions or torches.

Amy Lynn Taylor (p. 105) lives nestled in the Collegiate Peaks of Buena Vista, Colorado with her husband, Robert. Their five grown children have all left home, so these days their boxer, Zugspitze, receives their undivided attention.

After 11 years as an elementary teacher, Amy stepped away from the classroom to focus on her writing although she still mentors and tutors young children.

A firm believer that learning should last a lifetime, Amy takes writing courses, attends writing conferences, and submits her work for critique.

When she's not working on her novels, writing a blog, or recording a vlog; Amy is reading (often several books at once), hiking a fourteener (a mountain over 14,000 feet) with Robert, riding her Peloton, cuddling with her dog, or sharing a great cup of coffee with a friend.

Marilyn Turk's (p. 69) roots are in the coastal South. She calls herself a "literary archaeologist" because she loves to discover stories hidden in history. She is the author of two World War II novels, and the Coastal Lights Legacy series set in 1800s Florida — *Rebel Light, Revealing Light, Redeeming Light, and Rekindled Light* — featuring lighthouse settings. Marilyn's novella, *The Wrong Survivor*, is in the Great Lakes Lighthouse Brides collection. Her novella, *Love's Cookin' at the Cowboy Cafe*, is part of the Crinoline Cowboys collection. She also writes for *Daily Guideposts*.

She lives in Florida with husband, Chuck, her grandson, and an antique cat. When not writing, Marilyn can be found playing tennis, gardening, walking, fishing, or kayaking. She and Chuck have visited over 100 lighthouses so far, but the RV is ready to go see more.

Website: @http://pathwayheart.com

Email: marilynturkwriter@yahoo.com

Kenneth Avon White (p. 56) resides in Charlotte, North Carolina. His business career centers around equipping employees to successfully adjust to workplace changes. He likens his presence on the job to the IRS's knocking on a person's door, in that people like change about as much as they enjoy taxes.

In the world of writing, however, Ken finds that change is welcomed. Plots and characters and places all adjust to an ever-changing landscape as stories unfold like a yellow brick road that leads to some place magical. Ken has had a series of meditations published in *The Upper Room* magazine, the next slated for late 2019. He is also published in several books in the *Short and Sweet* series. In his spare time Ken takes in the arts, volunteers, and referees the voices in his head competing to tell the next story.

An avid reader, **Kim Wilch** (p. 116) longed to write a book of her own. With colorful family characters and no direction, she took writing classes. Kim has begun the journey to write a memoir that is both painful and jaw-droppingly ridiculous. She joined a writing group that encourages submissions of short stories and is a recent winner of the Bess Streeter Aldrich Contest.

A wife, mom, and proud grandma from Nebraska; Kim enjoys camping, traveling, crafting, and giving her puppies belly rubs. Often, she can be found in her garden or with a camera in her hand. Kim enjoys volunteering and helping others; she paints on windows at an Alzheimer's facility, takes calls at the crisis center, mentors for TeamMates, and scrapbooks for Make a Wish.

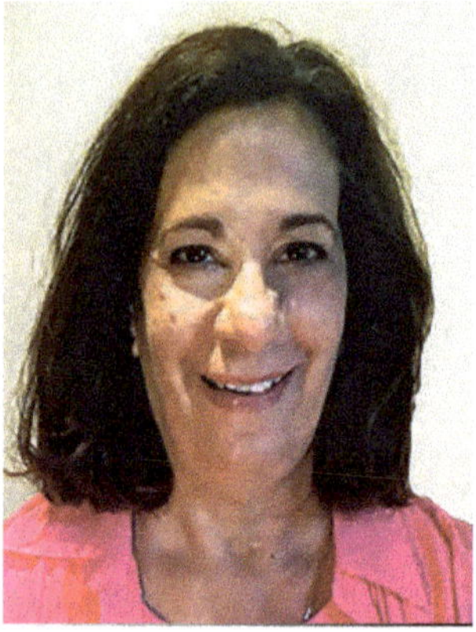

Andrea Woronick (p. 23) lives in New England with her husband, Mike, and their dog, Ruppert. When her children, Monica and Jeff, were born Andrea gave up her job in medical research. After that she got involved with volunteering in her children's schools and in her church. When her children were grown, she accepted a position as Director of Faith Formation at her church where she was responsible for creating content, overseeing and teaching children and adults, and leading retreats.

Since leaving her position, Andrea spends her time volunteering at a non-profit medical children's charity and playing piano at various facilities for senior citizens. In her spare time Andrea loves to read, take long walks, and spend time in prayer — thanking God for the many blessings in her life.

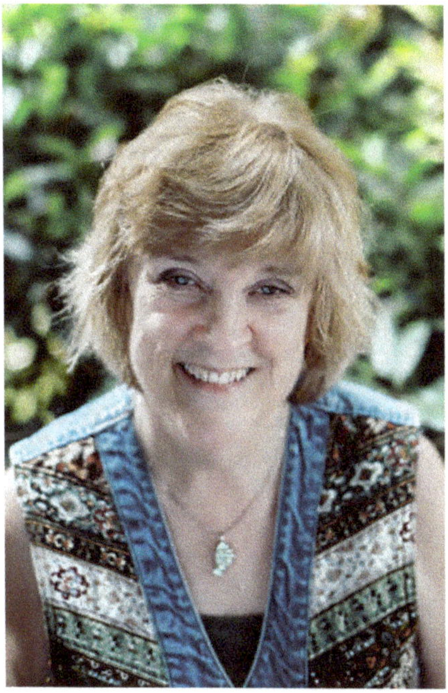

Susan Cheeves King

For nearly 25 years, Susan Cheeves King served with *The Upper Room,* a daily-devotional magazine with millions of readers circulated in over 100 countries in 35 languages. Currently she is continuing what she began in her role as Associate Editor: speaking at Christian writers' conferences in the U.S. and Canada. Her professional life has also included teaching English and feature-writing classes at Lipscomb University, Biola University, and Abilene Christian University for a total of over 27 years. Early in her career, she served as book editor and radio-program producer/on-air talent for The Institute of Scriptural Psychology, wrote magazine features as a freelance writer, and functioned as a seminar facilitator in leadership and group dynamics. Susan and husband, Joe, live in Franklin, Tennessee, and have three grown children, two grandchildren, two foster grandchildren, and two "grandchildren-in-law."

www.ingramcontent.com/pod-product-compliance
Lightning Source LLC
Chambersburg PA
CBHW051209090426
42740CB00021B/3432
* 9 7 8 1 6 0 4 9 5 0 5 7 1 *